MW00698010

Faulkner and
the Novelistic
Imagination

Robert Dale Parker

Faulkner and the Novelistic Imagination

UNIVERSITY OF ILLINOIS PRESS
Urbana and Chicago

Publication of this work was supported in part
by a grant from the Andrew W. Mellon Foundation.

This book is printed on acid-free paper.

Library of Congress Cataloging in Publication Data

Parker, Robert Dale, 1953–
    Faulkner and the novelistic imagination.

    Includes index.
    1. Faulkner, William, 1897–1962—Criticism and interpretation.
I. Title.
PS3511.A86Z945   1985   813'.52   84-2519
ISBN 0-252-01155-4 (alk. paper)

*in memory of Faye B. Parker
and in honor of Theodore E. Parker*

Contents

Acknowledgments

I thank the friends and colleagues who have warmly encouraged this study and generously criticized portions or versions of its many revisions, especially R. W. B. Lewis and Richard Brodhead, as well as Charles Feidelson, Arthur Kinney, Brian McHale, and Robert Stepto. To all of them, and the many others who have aided this work and the spirits of its author, I am deeply grateful.

CHAPTER 1

Something Happening: Faulkner and the Novelistic Imagination

What is it like to read a Faulkner novel? Miss Rosa Coldfield knows. Her problem is not so much frustration as deprivation: she never gets the facts.

> I remember how as we carried him down the stairs and out to the waiting wagon I tried to take the full weight of the coffin to prove to myself that he was really in it. And I could not tell. I was one of his pallbearers, yet I could not, would not believe something which I knew could not but be so. Because I never saw him. You see? There are some things which happen to us which the intelligence and the senses refuse . . . —occurrences which stop us dead as though by some impalpable intervention, like a sheet of glass through which we watch all subsequent events transpire as though in a soundless vacuum.[1]

Rosa refuses to believe "something" (she can hardly say by what other word to call it) that she nevertheless knows: the fact of Charles Bon. She has seen his effects on the Sutpens, including her sister and niece and nephew, but she has never seen him, cannot be sure he really lies in his coffin, though she carries it herself. And neither can we the readers be sure. Reading Faulkner, we often cannot tell whether we read a story of events, or a non-story of the conspicuous lack of events, so much seems to be made of so little. Yet what we do not see controls what we do see, recognizably but almost invisibly, "like a sheet of glass through which we watch all subsequent events."

Within the fiction, we may presume, the facts must somehow finally be ascertainable, as in a detective novel. Either there was a

1

Charles Bon, or there was not. We see a letter (though unsigned) and later a tombstone (with birthdate and place wrong), and we suppose they show, however precariously, that there must have been a Bon. And Bon either was or was not in the coffin—we never learn for sure which, but at least we trust it was one or the other. Somewhere concealed in the fiction the facts either can be found or could have been found by the characters, if they had looked. Faulkner, we may come to think, can be figured out.

Shreve McCannon disagrees. "'Wait,'" he protests to Quentin Compson, who in *Absalom, Absalom!* as in *The Sound and the Fury* would rather have facts—and judgments—definite.

> "Wait. Listen. I'm not trying to be funny, smart. I just want to understand it if I can and I don't know how to say it better. Because it's something my people haven't got. Or if we have got it, it all happened long ago across the water and so now there aint anything to look at every day to remind us of it. We dont live among defeated grandfathers and freed slaves (or have I got it backward and was it your folks that are free and the niggers that lost?) and bullets in the dining room table and such, to be always reminding us to never forget. What is it? something you live and breathe in like air? a kind of vacuum filled with wraithlike and indomitable anger and pride and glory at and in happenings that occurred and ceased fifty years ago? a kind of entailed birthright father and son and father and son of never forgiving General Sherman, so that forevermore as long as your childrens' [*sic*] children produce children you wont be anything but a descendant of a long line of colonels killed in Pickett's charge at Manassass?"
>
> "Gettysburg," Quentin said. [361]

Shreve would like—or so he here pretends—secure facts, leading to secure interpretations, but he cannot believe they are possible. For Shreve facts are flexible, so much so that they become funny. Is it the blacks who were freed, he asks, or the whites? He mocks Quentin's need for definite facts, since, to Shreve, Pickett might have served lugubrious legend equally well had he charged at Manassas instead of Gettysburg. In the same fashion, he elsewhere reverses Quentin's account of Bon saving the wounded Henry Sutpen, to make Henry save a wounded Bon; and another time he pokes fun at the Jefferson townspeople's awestruck taletelling and Thomas Sutpen's aristocratic pretensions by changing the story of

Sutpen's four luxury-laden wagons (44) to six wagons filled with "'crystal tapestries and . . . Wedgwood chairs'" (178). To Shreve, facts are but interchangeable fictions. Even his name has two versions, McCannon in the *Absalom* genealogy and MacKenzie in *The Sound and the Fury*, with never a reason to say one is more right than the other.

Whereas to Rosa particular facts are not known, and yet they mysteriously color everything, to Shreve facts, often the same ones that elude Rosa, are available, but they tell us nothing, not even that they can be trusted in themselves, let alone in what they imply about other things. Rosa's ignorance is tactical, she lacks a piece from the puzzle; Shreve's is epistemological, he has the most important pieces but refuses to trust them.

Radical ignorance, be it tactical like Rosa's or epistemological like Shreve's, is the distinctive problem Faulkner imposes on his readers. Indeed, Faulkner's novels are shaped as novels, as sustained narratives, by their elaborate orchestration of that ignorance. The main thing we know reading Faulkner is that we don't know the main thing, whether it is a fact, as for Rosa, or at the last an understanding of whether facts are possible, as for Shreve.

Yet Faulkner keeps pointing our attention to the very main thing we don't know. Like Rosa and Shreve, he calls it "something," a natural word, whether consciously chosen or not, for a focus of attention identifiable but not definable, an even homely word that nonetheless grows to tantalize by the bland way it keeps labeling the key thing that we do not know, without helping us come to know it. At the central moment in *Sanctuary*, Temple Drake repeatedly says that something—she never says what—is happening to her. Joe Christmas, approaching his key moment, repeatedly thinks his problem is that something is going to happen to him. Thomas Sutpen knows that something already has happened. Gradually, in each work, this taunting play of ignorance and knowledge signaled by the word "something" unfolds into a more broadly novelistic strategy of intricately woven mystery that, once observed, can be seen to control the best of Faulkner's novels with a continuous narrative, the four Yoknapatawpha novels published from 1930 to 1936.

The special claim of this book is that each of these four novels is told and twisted around a single event, and yet that that event, even as it determines nearly all we read, is defiantly withheld, at first epistemologically, then in *Sanctuary* tactically, and then both ways.[2] Thus the patterns of withheld somethings not only shape the individual novels, they also respond to each other and develop from one novel to another, each work testing different possibilities, until all the various strands come together in *Absalom, Absalom!*, which serves as climax and capstone to the process and becomes, formally, almost the latent goal of the three earlier novels.

In *Absalom, Absalom!* the great withheld something, as we will see in considerable detail, is what Faulkner skips over between Chapters V and VI: Quentin's discovery of Henry Sutpen and of Henry's motive or motives for murdering Charles Bon. Everything in the novel aims toward or derives from that one event, even though the event itself is missing (like Addie Bundren's adultery or Popeye's corn-cob or Joe Christmas's motives) until nearly the novel's end. At the same time, almost all the novel ostentatiously points to that event's determining significance, taunting and teasing us so as to drive us all the more to want what it refuses to give.

Even when *Absalom*'s withheld information is at last revealed, we win each revelation only at the cost of some yet more protracted withholding. Indeed, we learn the facts, or what seem to be the facts, by coyly staggered installments that force us to contemplate matters at great length in utter bewilderment, or in the but slightly more enlightened confidence of knowledge that turns out to be fatally incomplete. We learn that Henry killed Bon, but no credible reason why. Next we learn that Quentin and Rosa are about to go to the old Sutpen mansion, because "something" is out there, but then suddenly the novel skips four months without telling what something Quentin learned when he went there. Then at last we think we discover why Henry killed Bon, to prevent incest, and in that sudden onset of new knowledge we reevaluate all we have read. Still later we discover that Henry's motive was not to prevent the incest but rather to prevent miscegenation, and yet again we must reevaluate all we have read. And then we learn yet another startling new fact, this time that Quentin learned about the incest and the miscegenation not merely by finding new information at the old Sutpen mansion, but also by finding the source of that information, Henry himself, risen from the past as if from the dead.

By giving us the revelations of incest and miscegenation separately, instead of together as Quentin learns them, the narrative reproduces for its readers not the pattern of Quentin's discovery but instead the more distant pattern of Henry's discovery. That is, it reenacts Thomas Sutpen's two-step revelation to Henry of Bon's parentage: his saying on Christmas Eve of 1860 that Charles Bon is his son by an earlier marriage, and his saying in 1865 that he put aside his first wife upon finding out that she was part black, meaning that Bon, the half-brother and prospective husband of Henry's sister, is part black too. But the discoveries of incest and miscegenation are of course only two of the long-withheld things Quentin learns on his visit to the Sutpen house, the third being Henry himself. By delaying for a third revelation the surprise that Henry is alive and has returned, Faulkner stretches even further the impact of that one withheld incident of Quentin's and Rosa's visit. The shock of finding Henry, like the earlier shocks of incest and miscegenation, becomes stronger by being brooded over separately and being saved from any muting it might suffer if joined to the other two surprises that it was joined to for Quentin. Hence a single three-revelation incident (Henry, incest, miscegenation) is transformed, by an elaborately arrayed sequence of withholding, into three separate incidents of narrative, each with its own revelation, allowing each to be weighed both on its own and also against the others, and immeasurably drawing out and intensifying the shock of the determining central event.

Moreover, that event, as split in three, recapitulates and seems to evolve from the three controlling withholdings of Faulkner's earlier great novels of sustained narrative, the three other novels we will here study. Specifically, incest and its relation to another form of forbidden love, adultery, are the tremorously repressed secrets of As I Lay Dying, around and through which the novel and its characters are shaped. As two-thirds of the way through As I Lay Dying we discover who is Jewel Bundren's father, so two-thirds of the way through Absalom we discover who is Charles Bon's father, and both discoveries make all the difference. Likewise, miscegenation, or the fear of it, and the viciousness that fear can lead to, directly (as in Henry's murder of Bon) or indirectly (as in Joe Christmas's murder of Joanna Burden), are the reverberating secrets of *Light in August*. For Faulkner withholds Joanna's murder, the central event around which the novel revolves, and never tells whether Joe is miscegenated in the first place, the antecedent and perhaps more central mystery upon which that revolving finally depends. And lastly, the sudden discovery of Henry concludes a pattern of staggered revelation that, as we will see, closely repeats *Sanctuary*'s detective-story structure of protracted secrecy and sudden upending disclosure, with Horace Benbow learning at Goodwin's trial the equivalent of what Quentin learns at the Sutpen mansion, each pivotal episode exposing different versions of illicit desire translated into murderous brutality.

The climactic appearance of Henry, however, is qualitatively different from that series of revelations in the earlier novels from which, in Faulkner's imagination, it seems to derive. Henry's appearance changes the rules—lifts the problem of motive from historical abstraction to immediately contemporary crisis, in which someone remains who is responsible for the murder the motive led to. Quentin's discovery of Henry is thus a much amplified version of Hightower's collision with Joe Christmas near the end of *Light in August*, where Hightower's effort to save Joe and thereby to extend his own newly reestablished contact with the world fails utterly, forcing us—and, in the next chapter, Hightower himself—to wonder whether for him, for Hightower, it might be too late. In *Sanctuary* the comparable meeting of linked opposites, a murderer and a contemplator, comes not at the end but rather at the very beginning, when Horace is confronted by Popeye, who simply stares at him across the spring for hours. In *Sanctuary*'s version, with no previously accumulated reservoir of issues and emotions, the result is almost incomprehensible. We know what to make of it no more than Horace does. But in *Light in August* Hightower knows. And, at the last, Quentin in *Absalom* knows, and his knowledge creates that problem of judgment with which the novel ends.

But had all three aspects of *Absalom*'s central revelation been unveiled together and in chronological sequence, in one concentrated surprise between what are now Chapters V and VI, like the surprise of Addie's adultery, then all that is now at stake through the second half of the novel, morally, formally, and imaginatively, could never have been. Instead, Faulkner combined the single controlling unveiling of *As I Lay Dying,* the staggered but no less controlling unveiling of *Sanctuary,* and the much more complicated and culturally searching flirtation with unveiling in *Light in August* that forces us to care about the judgment more than the facts, combined all these startling visions of what a novel might do into one new novel that shows us how to read the others, that salutes, sustains, and surpasses them, celebrating, like no other work, its own imagination.

So intricate a procedure implies a particularly devious conception of how novels might work in the first place. Faulkner sensed that the fascination of mystery lies not in mere default, in absence, but rather in the active consciousness of absence, which is itself a form of presence. Hence the expectation of a delayed or withheld event can be itself an event, a crucial narrative fact out of which Henry James constructed an entire *nouvelle,* "The Beast in the Jungle." Faulkner delighted in exploiting that same fact, in and out of his writing. Joseph Blotner tells about a storytelling game Faulkner occasionally played at parties, probably derived from Twain's piece about Jim Blaine and his grandfather's ram in *Roughing It.* Faulkner and a friend in on the joke would corner some worshiper of novelists, and Faulkner would tell the most boring story he could imagine, without ever reaching the supposed point, the object being to see how long it would take their victim, who would expect the story to lead somewhere, to give up and find an excuse to walk away. That insistence that a story will eventually make sense, and the paranoia that such insistence implies, are the premises of Thomas Pynchon's novels; for "excluded middles," as Oedipa Maas of *The Crying of Lot 49* thinks, are "bad shit."[3] But we are stuck with them nonetheless.

Since everything cannot be told, and even what is told cannot be told all at once, all reading becomes an interaction between expectation and the violation of expectation, between expectation and surprise. As we read, we select details from which we construct hypotheses, and as we read more and gain more evidence, filling in some of the gaps (while creating new ones), we constantly revise those hypotheses, so that the work of reading continuously alternates between inductive and deductive reasoning.[4] Thus, to study the reading of gaps and withholding in narrative is but to study a larger and therefore clearer manifestation of what we do at every moment of reading.

The hypotheses we form as readers tell as much about us—because it is we who form them—as they do about the text. We therefore become responsible for, even implicated by, what we select—implicated by our own expectations and our own surprises. Hence the gaps that disturb us in Faulkner, a gap being one kind of surprise writ large, elide disturbing events that we have come to expect and, in effect, to want within the story. And by reminding or accusing us of that desire, the unexpected skipping over of such events may make us feel vicariously guilty of them; or at least it should make us wonder what they mean to us, whether that meaning comes through their presence or their absence.

Accordingly, much of the role that withholding plays in narrative derives from the principle that ignorance leads to wonder, as classically propounded by Henry James in his preface to "The Turn of the Screw," where he explains his purpose for avoiding anticlimactic "weak specifications," for not letting us know what "really" happened.[5] Less classically, but demonstrating the same principle, Gavin Stevens in *The Mansion* scribbles to Linda Snopes Kohl his reason for never having slept with her mother: *"Maybe it was because I wasnt worthy of her & we both knew it but I thought if we didnt maybe she might always think maybe I might have been."*[6]

The respective subjects of Gavin's confession and James's theorizing can help suggest the differences between Faulkner's and James's withholding.[7] Those differences lie in the two novelists' contrasting theaters of effect. James's is what has been variously called the theater, the melodrama, or the ordeal of *consciousness;* and the force of his effects without causes comes from the disarming intensity and near exclusiveness of attention in so epistemologically abstract a realm. Faulkner, with characters such as Darl Bundren and Gail Hightower, does not forgo the theater of consciousness, but he includes with as least as much intensity, and for some characters with as much exclusivity, a theater of an altogether opposed form of melodrama, of outrageously lurid *event*. Whereas in "The Beast in the Jungle" John Marcher's long-anticipated event turns out to be the lack of any event at all, with Joe Christmas or even more with Thomas Sutpen we are liable to be amazed at the power of lurid tactical event to exclude consciousness.

In James the fact of fascination tends to be more important than its object, even though that very preference is often the source of tragedy. The effort to find out, to fill in the gaps, is no more important in James than in Faulkner, but, as opposed to the actual finding out, it is proportionately much more important; for in Faulkner the actual facts—the adultery or the corn-cob or the murder or the motives for murder—play a larger role, are more specific and more central (especially if and when they are at last revealed). What counts most in James is the impetus to inference. What counts most in Faulkner is the impetus to inference, and the inference itself.

In that sense James is closer to Melville than to Faulkner, though he stops far short of the radical epistemological uncertainty of *The Confidence-Man,* or of Pynchon. When Steelkilt in "The Town-Ho's Story" of *Moby-Dick* whispers "something" to the men who are about to flog him, and his whispers have such paralyzing effect, how much less alluring and mysterious it would be were we told that he muttered, for example, something like "Beware for the sake of . . .," filling in the names of his enemies' wives. We never get the facts in *Moby-Dick,* or in much of James (archetypally "The Turn of the Screw"), but we usually get the facts—at least the most important ones—in Faulkner. Even, I will contend, in *Absalom, Absalom!*

To note whether we ever get the facts is one way to distinguish between different types of withholding. Gaps, however, can be differentiated not only by whether they are ever filled, but also by what kind of difference they make whether they finally are filled or not, as we have seen in *Absalom, Absalom!* There gaps may be either tactical or epistemological, depending on who perceives them. Still, *Absalom* brings together sensibilities that remain separate in some of the other novels, novels that find room of any considerable scale for only one mode of mystery. Thus we can differentiate the kind of withholding in *As I Lay Dying* from that in *Sanctuary* by contrasting the one's secrets or gaps of tactical significance, such as the withholding of how the impotent Popeye rapes Temple Drake, with the other's more mysterious secrets of epistemological significance, such as the withholding or obfuscating of why the Bundrens undertake their bizarre journey, and of what that may have to do with Addie's hidden adultery. But we must keep in mind that epistemological uncertainty in Faulkner always falls short of being absolute.[8] We do, for all practical purposes, know some things, whereas in *The Crying of Lot 49* we do not; and the interest in practical purposes is crucial. Both in Faulkner and in Conrad, his nearest precursor in narrative uncertainty, particular problems remain: What should Lord Jim or Emily Gould or Razumov, or Quentin, Darl, Hightower, or Henry Sutpen, *do?* Even though they are fictional, what they can do depends on how and what they can know. Mysteries must be acted upon, even as they remain mysteries.

Faulkner's subject, therefore, to the limited extent that we can reduce his many and varied experiments to a subject, is the ethical dilemma that arises from the problematic (or sometimes, as in *Sanctuary*, frighteningly unproblematic) status of knowledge. For not only are his novels difficult to understand; they also tend to be about the difficulty of understanding itself, and about the problems engendered by that difficulty, for both the characters and the readers. Typically, as things start getting out of control, one Faulkner character pleads to another that they "Wait!"[9]—as if by slowing time they might somehow catch up with it, as we sometimes slow our reading even while the momentum of Faulkner's sentences surges forward. Faulkner's loosely Bergsonian notion that one time—the present—can contain all times,[10] his vision, that is, of synchronic perception like Benjy's in *The Sound and the Fury*, is continuously fighting a losing battle against diachrony, against narrative, against the inevitability of sequence; and in the exploitation of that battle he develops most of what makes his writing difficult.

Faulkner seems to take difficulty for granted. For him it cannot be countered with a "Notes on 'The Waste Land'" or a schema to

Ulysses. It is neither a modernist riddle nor a post-modernist toy. It is closer to Hawthorne's or Melville's elaborations of ambiguity, but—among other things—reading Joyce and Eliot and especially Conrad helped Faulkner build his own mode of difficulty, one more directly embedded in social and psychological phenomena than that of any of these several predecessors.

Thus Faulkner, through the particular nature of his difficulty, manages to be modern without for the most part being modern*ist.* Modern*ism* suggests Pound, Eliot, and Joyce, with whom Faulkner is often grouped.[11] But the term in itself does embarrassingly little to define what it labels, only identifying it as current or recent. Perhaps the one thing we can say most certainly about modernism is that, from a dozen varying motives, it is difficult; and difficulty seems to be much (granted, not all) of the reason that Faulkner has been associated with it. "I have written a poem so modern," Faulkner wrote to his mother in 1925, "that I dont know myself what it means." T. S. Eliot proclaimed the doctrine in his famous 1921 essay on metaphysical poetry: "We can only say that it appears likely that poets in our civilization, as it exists at present, must be *difficult.* Our civilization comprehends great variety and complexity, and this variety and complexity, playing upon a refined sensibility, must produce various and complex results. The poet must become more and more comprehensive, more allusive, more indirect, in order to force, to dislocate if necessary, language into his meaning."[12] Difficulty as essential to modernism was transported by modernist poets like Eliot from French symbolist and English metaphysical poetry, and transported from modern poetry to modern narrative. But narrative (as was already being shown by Conrad and Proust, from whom Eliot was learning: these relations are more tangled than any schema) inherently offers forms of difficulty different from those of poetry. Modernist poetry cultivates difficulty partly by disrupting the syntax of its sentences. Sentences are similarly disrupted in modernist fiction, but in fiction we have also a syntax of narrative, and in the modernists that too is disrupted, twisted and gapped—a formal change that, like the formal changes of modernist poetry, carries vast semantic consequences.

Gaps in narrative syntax, according to whether they are tactical or epistemological, lead the text in either of two directions: radically toward cohesion, as in a detective novel, or radically against it, as in *Ulysses*. Disorder made of other things than gaps, such as Joyce's protean typography, can be more multiform, hovering in between the two poles of clarifying and confusing. We tend to think of modernism in terms of the two less orderly of these three alternatives, in terms of the hovering in between and the radically disordered, forgetting or hardly caring that even *Ulysses* has, after all, a plot. Perhaps simple disorder and the active flight from order are indeed among those things that define modern*ism,* but they are far less typical of the more generally modern, if we include as modern, for example, Forster or Lawrence, Frost or Hemingway or Faulkner. The modern knows disorder but rarely risks—as, say, Eliot or Pound or Joyce risks—seeming craven before it. On the contrary, the modern sometimes knows order as only those traumatized by disorder can—as Horace Benbow, at the last, knows order.

Hence the order of the modern is order against the odds, or even, instead of the Victorian order of triumph, the more chastened order—as for Horace or Quentin—of certain defeat. *Middlemarch,* for example, as a genealogy of its characters will prove (my version shows over fifty, all of them related), is emphatically an ordered book. So is *Absalom, Absalom!* Yet it makes a more powerful and more frightfully precarious vision for Faulkner to salvage order in *Absalom,* where he must contain Rosa and Shreve, than for George Eliot to sustain it in *Middlemarch;* even though the order of *Middlemarch* dares at least to try to be more bluntly satisfying than anything the more modern Faulkner would come near to (when not joking, as in *The Reivers).*

After Henry James our great novelists were too sophisticated and self-conscious to risk George Eliot's kind of daring. They exchanged the Victorian will to plot and shape with the modernist, Joycean will to misshape. And if modernism through Henry James and James Joyce heralded the demise of plot in favor of consciousness and technical virtuosity, then Faulkner took the same techniques he learned from modernism and, applying them with melodramatic selectivity, joined them to the new taking for granted of Freud, to the gothic, to romance and to the nineteenth-century American romance-novel tradition, all so as to resuscitate plot. In the process he retained, if no longer (after *The Sound and the Fury*) modernism, then at least the self-consciously modern that modernism so vociferously ushered in. And that capacity for provocative selection, at the origin of novels built around momentous mysteries and appalling absences, is itself peculiarly modern, with deep roots in the growth of broadly modern modes of perception.

To understand those modes of perception as they relate to Faulkner's selectivity, it may help to digress briefly. Through mass literacy, visual and literary realism, and the ubiquitous immediacy of mass communications, we have come to accept as routine an intensity of presence previously inconceivable, so that John Fowles, meditating on the relation between such changes and the form of novels, can nostalgically lament (rephrasing Wordsworth) that "The world is only literally too much with us now."[13] Indeed, each day's events can be screened in our living rooms with the seeming objectivity of a machine's eye. The familiarity of so capacious a presence, not only through television but also through photography, film, and radio, closes certain formal and social possibilities, as Fowles complains; but it also opens others. It permits us to learn as much from Hemingway's sparing hints as we could before from Cooper's unending itemizations. In painting, the pre-Raphaelites responded to those changes with an anti-photographic (and therefore made possible by photography) deep focus. If we thought we knew what we knew, then they would show us that we knew even more. In the other direction, developing both from realism and from Manet with his shallow focus, the impressionists trusted what we knew in common and gave us what they particularly knew. Similarly, in literature, moving some ten to fifty years behind painting, came the realists, who surprised us by pointing to the breadth of our common perception: Flaubert, George Eliot, Zola, Dreiser; and then the counterrealists, we might call them, or really the second-generation realists, such as Proust and Joyce, who could take for granted our common perception to the point where they sometimes seem almost to be writing, as the impressionists seem to be painting, for themselves. They leave out, make gaps of, the preliminaries, the transitions, "realistically" mimicking the way we leave such matters out in thinking to ourselves, so that we not only *need* desperately to reconstruct and fill in, but also we *can*—the mimicry is just enough recognizable.

Faulkner, formally another generation or half-generation along, assuming rather than discovering Freud and having absorbed the as if Freudian tradition of mystery in Poe, Hawthorne, and Melville (to which his cherished Conrad so easily fits), could choose a different sort of leaving out, a different sort of gap, because with such examples before him he could more readily find literary capital in narrative repression. The time might seem to have been ripe for that repression or death of plot given momentum by Joyce, for the refusal of ordinarily progressing sequence. Yet mystery's confusion always implies at least the potential for its resolution. Where we have an Ishmael, who can make no sense, no understandable plot, of the white whale (as Shreve can make none of the Sutpens), we always might find a Dupin or a Gavin Stevens, who can make nothing but sense, who reveals a plot where before we saw none. And Faulkner, raised by his father and mammy into a strong tradition of oral storytelling, and by his mother on Shakespeare and detective fiction, always relished a good plot. His own plots, then, became more artful versions of detective novels, became the conscious plottings or progressions of deceitful counterplots, or repressions. The ubiquitous perception of modern art and mass media thus gave Faulkner wider options. He could cultivate the newly enhanced taste for fulsome realism—and surely he is one of our language's great describers. At the same time, because his readers had come to think they knew so well what to expect, he could the more audaciously and selectively withhold.

Modern painting, after impressionism, developed along often comparable lines. Responding to Cézanne (one of Faulkner's favorites[14]), artists developed ever more radical strategies of selection, from the cubist to the surreal. Painters like Dali or Magritte brought a simple surrealism of ultra-selection, as contrasted to what, in their distant predecessors Bosch or Brueghel (in his Bosch-like works), might be called a surrealism of surfeit. Similarly, whereas withholding in Proust and Joyce and the more Joycean *The Sound and the Fury* is so profuse (like the wild, unselective energy of Bosch) that it usually has to be the medium through which every detail cannot help being seen, in Faulkner's novels after *The Sound and the Fury* the withholding is more local, more concentrated. That concentration, that conserving and parceling out, at first keeps us from seeing how what we read is implicated by what we do not read. We must work to discover how, and part of the discovery is in the sudden concentrated upset, the chilling reorientation of surprise, as we are told abruptly about Addie's adultery, or Popeye's corn-cob, or Charles Bon's parentage, and so find that we must struggle to see anew things we had assumed we already understood.

Faulkner more than anyone else merged these modernist techniques of formal complication and symbolic selection with comparably intricate, specifically American traditions.[15] Classic American fiction, Poe, Hawthorne, and Melville, has long been noted for its tendency toward psychologically pregnant selection over broadly inclusive social depiction, a tendency developed partly in response to the fierce repressions and individualist license of American Puritanism, which for Faulkner was still very much alive. Critics have often traced the Puritanism in Faulkner's novels—Whitfield, the Burdens, McEachern, Doc Hines, Goodhue Coldfield—yet perhaps we can see it not only as a set of realistically portrayed circumstances and characters, but also as a formally determinant pattern of thought. For the novels choose not just anything to withhold and repress; they choose their most frightening sins, the same sorts of things people repress. And, as in people, the novel's repressions govern the shape of those things that remain unrepressed: nothing moves Addie's family more than the emotional repercussions of an adultery they have never even been told happened. Thus to read Faulkner's novels as shaped by the screen of their withholdings is in a sense to psychoanalyze them, or, in American cultural terms, to see in their form the same kind of psychological history we might see in a Puritan diary or conversion narrative, the same struggle of secret sin against confession, whether it be in a real Puritan narrative or in what survives from the habits of thought those narratives represent, in which the intensity of secret sin only increases the urge to pry into and expose it. For the more a tale prolongs its secrets, the more it

provocatively points to the existence of something that it needs to be secretive about. Such habits of mind survive literarily in Poe and Melville, whom Faulkner read avidly, and especially in Hawthorne, whose *The Scarlet Letter* is a model for *As I Lay Dying.* More important, those same ways of thinking profoundly touched Faulkner's extraliterary experience, growing up amidst southern Calvinism, being hauled off to revival camp every summer as a child, and later, for example, being specially denounced from the pulpit because the minister thought he drank too much to continue as volunteer scoutmaster. ("'They're just Baptists,'" Miss Jenny tells Horace when a Jefferson preacher similarly denounces Lee Goodwin.[16])

Closely related, in Faulkner's inherited Americanness, is the idea of the New World that Ike McCaslin and McCaslin Edmonds debate in *Go Down, Moses,* the idea of an American, edenically fresh start, an optimism that can easily turn over into appalled despair, as when Horace believes he can bring about justice and discovers he has made things unimaginably more horrible, or when Hightower's idyllically envisioned Jefferson collapses into a solipsistic parody of his hopes. To have to discover evil, as Horace and Hightower do, is to make things worse by having refused to see it in the first place, which is exactly the position these novels force on us as readers, making the worst things seem even worse by concealing them for so long. Thus Ike McCaslin's vision of a lost American Eden is the tale of a mistake that, by being repressed, is transformed into a license for crime, the history of a contrived innocence that coerces us to evade and repress yet more the horrors we will nevertheless discover in ourselves. And because they are more repressed, they become more powerful when suddenly they burst forth in some other form, as when Ike reads the old plantation ledgers or meets Roth Edmonds's deserted lover, or, more immediately, when Goodwin is brutalized and burned. The reverse side of that American idealism, part of the bursting forth, is the modern sense of belatedness and hopelessness, a sense which excuses formal anarchy or disorder and permits a newly frank repertoire of horrors, such as the mutilating of Addie, Temple, Goodwin, and Joe Christmas. Faulkner first makes that repertoire his own and then subjects it to a secondary order, the reasserting order of revealed withholding, whereby we do not learn the worst about what happens to Temple until the last, when it can mean the most.

Thus each of the novels discussed here has, at the last, a definite order, a hidden but discoverable shape. "Each book had to have a design," Faulkner once said, as another time he insisted "that a novel has set rules."[17] In the four novels studied here the set rules say that each book tells and sustains its story by repressing that story's key elements. To some extent this is true of any narrative that does not begin by revealing its ending. But Faulkner's withholding, as by now must be apparent, involves far more than just delay. His novels' movement from tactical somethings to epistemological somethings, from individual secrets to a larger and more pervasive secrecy, is the movement from the frequent statement that "something" conspicuously indefinite "happened" or "is going to happen" to the sense that, because the indefiniteness of the something is so extreme or prolonged, something more radically indefinite *is* happening.

Some of this process emerges in Faulkner's first mature novel, *The Sound and the Fury* (1929), in which he discovered solutions to the problems of form that had almost kept his preceding novel, *Flags in the Dust* (also 1929, with its title changed to *Sartoris*), from being published. As Faulkner himself told the story a few years later:

> The first publisher to whom I submitted [the] 600 odd pages of mss. refused it on the ground that it was chaotic, without head or tail. I was shocked. . . . I showed the mss to a number of friends, who told me the same general thing—that the book lacked any form whatever; at last one of them took it to another publisher, who proposed to edit it enough to see just what was there.
>
> . . . I [argued] hotly with the person designated to edit the mss. . . . I said, "A cabbage has grown, matured. You look at that cabbage; it is not symmetrical; you say, I will trim this cabbage off and make it art; I will make it resemble a peacock or a pagoda or 3 doughnuts. Very good, I say; you do that, then the cabbage will be dead."
>
> . . . "The trouble is," he said, "Is that you had about 6 books in

here. You were trying to write them all at once." He showed me what he meant, what he had done, and I realised for the first time that I had done better than I knew and the long work I had had to create opened before me and I . . . wondered if I had invented the world to which I should give life or if it had invented me, giving me an illusion of greatness[.][18]

Faulkner here looks back on the same sprawling energy of *Flags in the Dust* that other people objected to and sees it as the source of his later works' greatness, the source not alone in subject—as the first completed Yoknapatawpha book—but even more so in its alleged chaos of form. To have the one book called six books trying to be written all at once seemed to him the highest possible compliment (he was at that time writing the four-part *The Sound and the Fury*); years later he would adopt a similar remark, that he was trying to say everything in one sentence, as a prideful staple to get him through interviews. The problem, though, is that when such diversity is compressed into such small compass, it raises special difficulties of novelistic form, difficulties that his friends, at least, felt made a failure of *Flags in the Dust*.

But when he raised those same difficulties again in *The Sound and the Fury*, he conquered them by what I would suggest was his personal discovery of two novel forms, two opposed strategies to exert form over a threatened chaos. One of those strategies was simply to concede the point, to make no pretense of continuity, and to divide the novel into four discontinuous sections. The other was exactly the opposite, that is, it was to turn the making no pretense of continuity into a mere pretense itself, for no one of those four ostensibly separate sections can be understood alone. Even the third and fourth sections, which seem so accessible after reading the first two, would seem vastly more obscure if—as some people have wished—they came first.[19]

The pitting against each other of two such opposed strategies makes each throw the other into high relief. Even in Benjy's section, where bewildered readers cannot help noticing the radical time shifts and discontinuities, they cannot help at least beginning to note also that the shifts from one time to another start to settle into a pattern and to fill in some of the same discontinuities that they force on us in the first place. The two general principles of form, in other words, soon become relatively obvious, freeing readers to concentrate their attention on the endless array of individual manifestations, the working through of which is not obvious at all.

Those two principles, the one of conceding the discontinuity of chaotic material and the other of trying to stitch the discontinuities back together, are the two principles that separately direct nearly the whole scheme of Faulkner's remaining novels. The present study, then, works from the assumption that, after *The Sound and the Fury*, Faulkner's novels can be divided into two groups, roughly separate chronologically, according to which of the two principles discovered in *The Sound and the Fury* most influences their overall shapes. Such divisions are of course a matter of degree, but the differentiations are broad. First, in *As I Lay Dying* (1930), *Sanctuary* (1931), *Light in August* (1932), and *Absalom, Absalom!* (1936), Faulkner shapes his novels by assuming the chaos of energy, the six books in one, and then trying to construct a form that can weave that chaos into a continuous whole. In the novels that follow he does just the opposite, again assuming the chaos of energy, the six novels in one, but this time conceding the issue of unity by dividing the novels (not all readers even grant that they should each still be called novels) into strongly discontinuous parts. Those books from the second group would be *The Unvanquished* (1938), *The Wild Palms* (1939), *Snopes* (the trilogy of *The Hamlet,* 1940; *The Town,* 1957; and *The Mansion,* 1959), *Go Down, Moses* (1942), *Intruder in the Dust* (1948) to the limited extent that it is a continuation of *Go Down, Moses,* and *Requiem for a Nun* (1951). (That leaves out only three novels, *Pylon, A Fable,* and *The Reivers,* from 1935, 1954, and 1962 respectively, each of which has in its own way already been acknowledged as something of an anomaly, though individual readers may prefer to group any of them in one category or another.)

The two principles that, by being pitted against each other in *The Sound and the Fury,* were there made relatively obvious, are made far more problematic in the later novels, where one or the other principle operates in comparative isolation. As a result, in the second group, critics have tended to see their task as the unveiling of a disguised unity—a dangerous (if sometimes necessary) task, because it risks replacing a book's admirably frustrating distinctiveness with the dubious critical prescription that art must be unified. On the other hand, my work here will be to show that in the earlier, more continuous novels the assumption that great art is necessarily continuous has tended, if only by comparison, to minimize notice of the full subtlety with which those novels' continuity is wrought from a six-plots-in-one chaos.

The specific method of that tenuously wrought continuity is to withhold. Such a method is of far less interest for full-scale critical exposition in *The Sound and the Fury* and the second set of novels because they so advertise their withholdings, their discontinuities, as to leave even the details of discontinuous method mostly self-evident. And so the novels chosen for study here are all from the first group (which it happens is, as a group, a better set of novels), all with narratives continuous but unsequential, so that we can both describe a phase in Faulkner's career and also study the working of unsequential but continuous narrative in general.

As I Lay Dying, the next novel after *The Sound and the Fury,* is the one that most resembles it, but has nevertheless a far more chronologically continuous narrative. *As I Lay Dying,* especially as it rests on Addie's crucial monologue and the withholding of that monologue for two-thirds of the book, is swayed by a drive to fuse, regardless of the inherent contradictions, things normally irreconcilable, be they Addie's and Anse's contrary attitudes toward language (as obstacle or vehicle) or the novel's outrageous, much-debated plot, at once heroic and absurd, grotesque and epic. Such apparent paradoxes subsume the many individual withholdings under a larger, epistemological uncertainty like that of *The Sound and the Fury,* though in the later work the secrecy seems less absolute, less resistant to critical scrutiny.

Faulkner's next novel, *Sanctuary,* was drafted before *As I Lay Dying* and revised after it. Because our interest is in these novels' larger structural ordering, and because it is just such larger patterns that Faulkner most revised, for our purposes *Sanctuary* must be considered as following *As I Lay Dying,* with which it has countless similarities of image and phrase. Otherwise, the two novels withhold in opposite ways. For in *Sanctuary* the status of knowledge is not in question. The world is known to be (or, depending on whose perspective we emphasize, discovered to be) a gruesome place; therefore the withholding is purely tactical, apparently in emulation of the detective novel, which explains evil doings but makes no pretense of explaining Evil itself.

Having thus developed two different sorts of withholdings for two different sorts of novels, Faulkner is then able, in *Light in August* and *Absalom, Absalom!*, to combine them to create something else again, to mix epistemological and tactical uncertainty and set them competing against each other. *Light in August* is so crowded with minor, tactically withheld somethings that in their cumulative effect they carry a suggestion of epistemological significance. It withholds as well a larger tactical something at its center: the murder of Joanna Burden. Also withheld are the facts about whether Joe Christmas has any black blood, facts which do not inherently hold epistemological significance but are taken to hold it by Joe and the people around him. As a result, withholding in *Light in August* becomes more largely and abstractly a withholding of definition, a resistance to typing characters by race or partly, I will suggest, by gender, and a resistance on such a large scale that it translates into the novel's refusal to type itself into any particular, inherited and organic notion of novelistic structure.

Absalom, Absalom!, by contrast, despite its seemingly overreaching rhetoric, is—as we have already begun to see—one of the most elaborately and precisely structured novels in the language, and with it our study will culminate. In *Absalom, Absalom!* Quentin Compson tries to figure out the story of the Sutpens, a story that revolves around a confrontation between Thomas Sutpen and his son Henry one Christmas Eve, when "something happened," though nobody knows what. Indeed, much of the novel recounts its various characters' efforts to re-confront Henry and make him tell what happened; and the entire narrative is structured around the central scene in which Quentin himself does just that, even while Faulkner refrains from giving us that scene.

The result is a novel so obsessively wrapped around one withheld and misrepresented event that it is usually read as I am suggesting *As I Lay Dying* should be read, as a sort of case study in epistemological uncertainty. But by accepting and expanding Cleanth Brooks's arguments about its narrative structure, I will emphasize not the uncertainty but instead the certainty that finally shocks us by being so outrageously specific. The confusion comes because the blend of vagueness like that in *The Sound and the Fury* and *As I Lay Dying* with uncertainty like that in *Sanctuary* creates a hybrid. For we finally get the outrageous specificity of *Absalom* only by the violence of coerced abstraction; that is, Henry's murder of Charles Bon because of Bon's fraction of black blood makes suddenly fatal an otherwise innocent genetic accident. As a result, by the end of *Absalom* we have a more peculiar sort of ineffability than I think anyone has yet suggested. Despite Shreve's playful doubting, we know all the important facts, but that very knowledge is Quentin's problem. For the only ineffability that remains is a moral one, the problem of what to do or believe on the basis of those facts. At the end, as the furious momentum of narrative finally halts, it is these issues, these ultimate epistemological dilemmas, that leave Quentin, and perhaps Faulkner, as if paralyzed ethically—and perhaps therefore narratively, novelistically.

CHAPTER 2

Something Secret and Selfish: *As I Lay Dying*

My ideas about *As I Lay Dying* are disparate, and in pursuit of a compensating clarity I want to begin by straightforwardly outlining them. I take the main fact about *As I Lay Dying*—after its beauty, about which I can say nothing very illuminating—to be its sheer strangeness. No reader fails to notice that strangeness, and yet critics have not done justice to it, despite some admirable efforts.[1] One way we resist the strangeness of *As I Lay Dying* and of Faulkner's work in general is to misread sometimes even the most basic facts. Such misreadings—and of course I have no way to know that I do not contribute my share of them—cannot much erode the patent strangeness of *The Sound and the Fury.* Few critics actually believe the simplification that Quentin's strange ability to recount his story up to the moment of his suicide can be explained away by the folk-wisdom notion that your whole life passes through your mind in a single moment just before death. Yet Addie's section in *As I Lay Dying* is often reductively explained in similar terms. While misreadings are common for many Faulkner novels,[2] for *As I Lay Dying* they are dominant.

For that reason I want to begin with practically a list, not by any means of every critical error, but of certain especially frequent misunderstandings. Some of my corrections may themselves be wrong, or perhaps I make some original contributions to our common nearsightedness. The point is not any claim to be more careful than anyone else; rather, it is to delineate the strangeness of *As I Lay Dying* in terms of the resistance that strangeness engenders

23

in us, its readers, as we try to reduce it to something more familiar.)
Then, having reviewed our frequent misunderstandings, I will try
to confront directly that strangeness and explore what we can
learn from our resistance to it, thereby (indirectly, perhaps) illuminating some of the beauty to which the strangeness is so closely
allied. After thus studying the novel's defining obfuscations and
enigmas and the considerable extent to which they resist explanation, I want then to examine the more traditional gestures that *As
I Lay Dying* does indeed make toward explanation, largely because those gestures carry interest in themselves, but also to avoid
a simplifying distortion and to lead us into *Sanctuary,* where
Faulkner turns from the novel of enigma sustained, as in *The
Sound and the Fury* and *As I Lay Dying,* toward the detective
novel, the novel specifically of enigma explained.

I. Frequent Misunderstandings

That the novel bears the marks of having been written quickly.
This notion is the legacy of Faulkner's tall tales about his writing
As I Lay Dying, tales that are a peculiar mixture of braggadocio,
false modesty, and self-deprecation.[3] If Faulkner's lies took a different tack, if he said he had struggled over the novel for years, we
could just as glibly identify the impressionistic marks of meticu-
lous labor. Whether or not we consider the three months or so
that he took to draft and revise *As I Lay Dying* to be a short time,
the number of days between first word and last period has nothing
to do with the degree of care Faulkner applied to his writing; nor
is it even meaningful to say that a fine novel written hastily was
not written carefully. A quantitative measure of care depends ultimately on a qualitative measure.[4] All this would be mere quibbling
(and perhaps it is) were it not for the supporting role it plays in so
many critical arguments. Critics find things in *As I Lay Dying* that
they do not like or understand, and they explain such things away
as the penalties of haste. But it cannot help to exempt as the result
of carelessness those things that seem to baffle description; for to
gloss over the sheer difficulty of describing a strange book is to
pretend it is not strange at all.

That Addie's making Anse promise to take her body to Jefferson is her revenge on him. Several critics have already refuted this idea.[5] Addie says she realizes "that I had been tricked by words older than Anse or love, and that the same word had tricked Anse too, and that my revenge would be that he would never know I was taking revenge. And when Darl was born I asked Anse to promise to take me back to Jefferson when I died, because I knew that father had been right."[6] Addie simply does not say what her revenge is; she does not even say that Anse is the object of it. If anything, the object of her revenge would seem to be not Anse, but whatever (perhaps the word "life"?) has tricked both her *and* Anse. She makes no connection between her revenge and Anse's promise other than to mention the one right after the other (she says "*And* when," not "So when"), which gives us no reason to say that the one *is* the other. Nor could she have known that carting her off to Jefferson would turn out to be so difficult that it could be considered revenge at all.

That Addie is masculine. The source of this misunderstanding seems to be some misread remarks by Cleanth Brooks. Brooks says Addie is more like the men in other Faulkner novels than she is like the women, and he notes a point of resemblance between her and the masculine Aunt Jenny of *The Unvanquished*. He never says Addie is masculine; in fact, he says quite the opposite.[7] Nevertheless, numerous critics have treated as common consensus the idea that Addie is somehow masculinized, twisted from her natural femininity (whatever that might mean). No doubt Addie is perplexing, perhaps perverse, but to question her gender identity is to avoid the problems she presents by putting other problems in their place.

Implicitly, and perhaps sometimes unwittingly, most discussions assume that Anse's and Addie's offspring are still children. One critic protested this practice over twenty-five years ago,[8] yet it continues through almost every essay. We need not assume that Faulkner had in mind an exact table of the Bundrens' ages, nor need we assume that if he did his book always abides by it. But we should recognize that, except for Vardaman, the Bundren siblings are not the "children" they are so often called. The actual statements about their ages, that Cash and Darl are roughly ten years older than Jewel, who three years ago was fifteen, and that Dewey Dell is seventeen (121, 190, 224, 246), together suggest that Jewel is about eighteen, Darl twenty-seven or -eight, and Cash twenty-eight or older. As in most of these examples, our natural desire to render the strange familiar makes us "explain" the Bundrens' strangeness by thinking of them as younger than the more direct evidence warrants, just as some critics have "explained" Vardaman's crazed grief by reading him as an idiot, as another Benjy.[9]

That Cash is somehow ennobled by the novel's end. Many recent critics have refuted this idea, but I still mention it because so many earlier critics advanced it. It is another way of turning the book into something easier to understand—in this case, a story of traditional character growth.

That for all practical purposes Darl, like Quentin Compson, has not had a mother. This notion derives from two of Darl's comments and their similarity to Quentin's repeated lament, *"if I'd just had a mother."*[10] Darl says, "I cannot love my mother because I have no mother. Jewel's mother is a horse" (89); later he says he has no mother "'Because if I had one, it is *was*. And if it was, it cant be *is*. Can it?'" (95). But no one seems to have noticed that, by the time Darl says he has no mother, he is literally right. Addie is dead. Although the act of pondering his mother's change from is to was leads Darl to question more intensely what sort of mother he once had, we never see him conclude, as Quentin does, that the sort of mother he had was in effect no mother at all. Instead, his questioning puts him in an in-between, unfamiliar state that we oversimplify by comparing him too closely to Quentin. He knows his mother is not what she was, and was not what he had desired. What she was instead, and therefore what she is in his memory, he does not know.

Darl intuits that Anse is not Jewel's father. From this many people assume *that Darl knows Jewel's father is Whitfield,* but for that there is no evidence. The oddity that generates our error is the seeming contradiction that Darl can see everything sometimes. The temptation is to reduce the oddity by remembering the clairvoyant power and forgetting that it is selective. Through most of the novel Darl knows all of Dewey Dell's thoughts (excepting only what she carries in the package), but only some of Addie's; and near the end he does not know his family is about to attack and incarcerate him.

That when the wagon tips over in the river, Jewel turns back to save Cash. I find no evidence for this. Though Cash cannot swim, it seems that Jewel goes back to save the coffin, as Cash seems to think in referring to Jewel's working "so to get her outen the river" (223). That Jewel would turn back for the coffin instead of for Cash makes no responsible sense—but neither, sometimes, does Jewel.

On the other hand, recognizing that the Bundrens sometimes make no sense does not give us license to read anything they do as senseless. It is often said, for example, *that Dewey Dell is bovine, and that she has some special sympathy with the Bundrens' cow.* Here the misogyny belongs not to Faulkner but to his critics. The cow follows her (59) for the same reason it followed Vardaman (54): it wants to be milked.

Similarly, many critics say *that MacGowan seduces Dewey Dell.* To seduce entails arousing sexual desire, but Dewey Dell has no desire for MacGowan. She makes a cold deal.

Doubtless some of these errors are trivial. The point is not to emphasize the individual errors, but instead to delineate the pattern, the attraction and convenience of error itself. Such a pattern would indeed be trivial were it only a configuration of niceties. But it is far more than that; for virtually all readings of *As I Lay Dying,* from absurdist to heroic, rest on a simplification of the Bundrens' motives, especially Anse's.

Though the exact mix varies from one discussion to another, we are repeatedly told *that Cash's motive to go to town is to buy a gramophone from Suratt, that the Bundrens care so little about Addie that by the end they forget her, and that Anse's grief is insincere, he does not love Addie, his only motive to go to town is to buy some teeth, or to buy teeth and get a new wife.* Such interpretations permit us to understand the seemingly incomprehensible by labeling it as, for example, absurdist, or burlesque, or mock or ironic-heroic. But as we shall see, all these readings are wrong, and as yet we have no label, and perhaps we cannot find a satisfactory one, for the strangeness they fail to describe.

We know that Cash means to buy a "graphophone" from Suratt, but nowhere is there any indication that he wants or needs to go to town for that. Indeed, what we know about Suratt (who is, in later books, renamed Ratliff) from other Yoknapatawpha material suggests quite the contrary, that Suratt would come to him. We have no cause to believe that Cash, like Jewel and for a while even Darl, goes to town for any reason other than to fulfill Addie's wish, an incomprehensible wish incomprehensibly abided by through the most adverse circumstances.

Granted, Tull suspects the Bundrens' motives. "Just going to town," he says. "Bent on it. They would risk the fire and the earth and the water and all just to eat a sack of bananas" (133). Either Tull speaks sarcastically (which, from the context, seems possible), or, in the absence of supporting evidence, we must reject his opinion. His commonsense perspective, which assumes that since there is no good reason then there must be no well-intentioned reason, misses the point; for the last thing the Bundrens have, especially in regard to Addie, is common sense.

Critics who think the Bundrens forget Addie by the end cite as evidence Anse's remarriage and Cash's, Dewey Dell's, and Vardaman's comfortable preoccupation with eating bananas. Put thus baldly the inadequacy of such reasoning grows all too apparent. It seems that, as readers, we have some special stake in denying that characters love when they express their love as peculiarly as do Darl, Dewey Dell, Cash, and especially Anse.

To deny Anse's love for Addie, strange as the comparison may otherwise sound, is like denying—as some critics have—Othello's love for Desdemona. It is radically to diminish the work, to forfeit the defining irreducible mystery in favor of the conveniently unremarkable. We can say that Othello loves not Desdemona but, instead, loves her love for him ("She lov'd me for the dangers I had pass'd,/And I lov'd her that she did pity them," I.iii); but in doing so we presumptuously conclude that, because we dislike the sort of love, the motive for love, therefore the emotion Othello says he feels ("I lov'd her") is not love at all. The same holds for our response to Anse's love—only more so, through the whole work, not just through two lines. We do not like Anse's love. It goes against what we want and preconceive love to be, and it does so not by any easily assimilable reversal, not by, for example, a sadistic twist to the familiar love-hate conundrum, but by something as mundane as it is strange. The peculiarity of Anse is that he is both so unfamiliar and so unspectacular at the same time. As long as we cling to readings that do away with that peculiarity by denying it, that lobotomize Anse by saying he does not love his wife or he goes to town just to get some teeth, we react to the difficulty by wishing it away.

The idea that Anse goes to town not for Addie but for teeth originates in the remark Darl envisions Anse making after Addie's death: "'God's will be done,' he says. 'Now I can get them teeth'" (51). By no means does this justify the critical consensus that Anse goes to town just to get teeth. He could easily bury Addie at New Hope and go to town for teeth after the high water subsides. True, Anse does not go to town often, so he might find Addie's wish a convenient excuse for a special trip. In fact, he has not been there once in the last twelve years (41). But that is his choice; the distance is far from prohibitive. The Tulls have just been there, and so has Jewel (7, 11, 38), so the journey seems routine enough not to require any special excuse. Furthermore, Anse continues on to Jefferson even after spending his teeth money to get a new team from Snopes, which—to the extent that we can prove anything in a fiction—proves his desire for new teeth to be a motive completely auxiliary.

Even without setting Darl's vision of Anse's remarks against the rest of the book, we can see from their own context that they do not mean Anse cares more for his teeth than for Addie. Addie, as Darl envisions the scene, has been dead for at least several minutes, enough time for Anse to have already spoken fourteen awkward sentences scattered over three pages. Dewey Dell, recovering from her initial shock, has left the room after pulling the quilt up to Addie's chin and smoothing it down.

> Pa stands over the bed, dangle-armed, humped, motionless. He raises his hand to his head, scouring his hair, listening to the saw. He comes nearer and rubs his hand, palm and back, on his thigh and lays it on her face and then on the hump of quilt where her hands are. He touches the quilt as he saw Dewey Dell do, trying to smoothe it up to the chin, but disarranging it instead. He tries to smoothe it again,

29

clumsily, his hand awkward as a claw, smoothing at the wrinkles which he made and which continue to emerge beneath his hand with perverse ubiquity, so that at last he desists, his hand falling to his side and stroking itself again, palm and back, on his thigh. The sound of the saw snores steadily into the room. Pa breathes with a quiet, rasping sound, mouthing the snuff against his gums. "God's will be done," he says. "Now I can get them teeth." [51]

Far from evidence of Anse's lovelessness, this passage—if we accept Darl's vision—seems evidence of anguished and grieving love, with his physical, hand-on-thigh display of sexual loss. Here is a man incompetent to express his love, reduced to a ridiculous mimicry of his daughter's gestural expressions of her love, and failing even at that. His failure, however, does not mean that he does not love. Instead, it shows both that his feelings are hopelessly inadequate, and that they are nevertheless unqualifiably real.

The only genuine cause to think that Anse does not love Addie is that she thinks he doesn't. She refuses to believe his professions of love. It seems that Addie's biases about language, and perhaps a fear of being loved, compounded with the sheer difficulty of comprehending Anse, lead her to underestimate his sincerity. Darl knows better, sees deeper, or at least—when his own biases do not interfere—more judiciously. He says of Anse, for example, "There is no sweat stain on his shirt. I have never seen a sweat stain on his shirt. He was sick once from working in the sun when he was twenty-two years old, and he tells people that if he ever sweats, he will die. I suppose he believes it" (16–17). Darl recognizes that Anse says things that are hard to believe, but he recognizes also, as Addie does not, that Anse himself believes them. Similarly, when Anse says he loves Addie, we may dislike or suspect what love means to him, but we cannot finally question that he does indeed love her. Anse's words may seem empty to Addie, but to him his word, his promise to her, means so much that it motivates the latter two-thirds of the novel's plot. And however cruelly Anse acts to his children, however ridiculous we find some of his protestations of love and grief for Addie (59, 74, 174), at times he achieves an eloquence that, if judging only from Addie's complaints, we would never expect: "'You all dont know,' pa says. 'The somebody you was young with and you growed old in her and she growed old in you, seeing the old coming on and it was the one somebody you could hear say it dont matter and know it was the truth outen the hard world and all a man's grief and trials. You all dont know'" (224; see also 218).

We can say that Anse is deluded about why his wife told him his growing old did not matter. We can even say that his love itself is deluded. But while these things may make us want to deny his love, the peculiarity of *As I Lay Dying* is that, at the same time, they do not give us the prerogative to do what we want. *As I Lay Dying* (like *The Sound and the Fury*) defies what we have come to expect novels to be. As traditional realistic fiction takes a familiar detail from nonfictional life and lavishes on it an attention that freshens, that defamiliarizes it, [11] so *As I Lay Dying* defamiliarizes the novelistic genre itself. By lavishing its odd sort of attention on familiar novelistic conventions, such as motive, it forces us to take a new look at those conventions, and at the novel itself, as a familiar thing made suddenly and troublingly strange.

II. The Strangeness of *As I Lay Dying*

Any reading is an interaction between text and reader, an interaction structured by its surprises, which give us a means to see the text as more than a reflection of the preconceptions we bring to it. If we take the surprises out, or contain them, or contort them into an expectable range of surprises, then we read too much as if we were looking into a mirror and we miss much of the chance to see the reader and the text in confrontation—miss, in other words, the chance to be changed into some different kind of reader.

Structuralists have described what I am calling the process of assimilating surprise as "naturalization" or "recuperation." [12] We respond to the unexpected, they point out, by explaining it, by naturalizing or recuperating it, by all the many activities that fall under the general rubric of interpretation. Two points are essential to structuralist ideas about naturalization and any critical application of them. The first is that it is impossible not to naturalize a text; we will always find some sort of reading or interpretation, even if only as a last resort to call a text nonsense, which is to naturalize it at the level of its being resistant to naturalization. The second point is our recourse against the first; it is that we can exercise deliberate control over the level at which we naturalize. We can and usually do naturalize a dustjacket blurb or a cookie recipe at the level of its lowest resistance, the easiest and most familiar level. But we can also choose to naturalize it at a less familiar, higher level, a level of greater resistance, reading it, for example, as an indication of larger social phenomena such as our culture's various cravings for mediated violence or unmediated sugar. In reading literature we make such choices all the time. We say that *Moby-Dick* is about a whaling voyage, or about the modes of human ambition, or about the possibilities of literary form. Or, in what some critics (including most structuralists) might regard as the highest and others as the lowest level of naturalization, we say it is about the energy of its own language. We may of course say any combination of these and other things, but some sorts of naturalization we will choose to emphasize more than others, and some sorts we will choose to exclude. Such choices become more problematic as the texts become more difficult, more inherently resistant to interpretation.

Thus we have tended—and it is a question of tendency, not of absolute error—to naturalize *As I Lay Dying* too easily, to rely on rather low or familiar orders of naturalization, whereas its strangeness calls for modes of naturalization unusually high or unfamiliar. One age's high level is another age's low level, so that to study naturalization is partly to study the history of literary— or, in this case, critical—taste. For example, in an influential 1923 essay T. S. Eliot praised Joyce for writing one text *(Ulysses)* on the substructure of another (the *Odyssey*), announcing, "Instead of narrative method, we may now use the mythical method."[13] Once revolutionary, Joyce's and Eliot's ideas about mythical method have since become cultural clichés. They are repeatedly applied to Faulkner and to *As I Lay Dying*, which we are told is deliberately another version of the Persephone myth (Cora Tull = Kora) or even of *The Waste Land* itself. Though the prevalence of such readings seems possible only after we accept that interpretation has become desperate, perhaps for works as baffling as *As I Lay Dying* we need more study of the impetus to desperation before we try to categorize it. The various categories that have been applied, such as comedy, epic journey, or mythical method, tell us more about the set of expectations that *As I Lay Dying* frustrates than they tell us about *As I Lay Dying* itself, or about how it raises and frustrates those expectations.

Vardaman's confused reaction to the story's events typifies the readers' predicament, much as does Shreve's amazement in *Absalom, Absalom!*, different as the two characters otherwise are. To assimilate what he cannot understand, the death of his mother, Vardaman transforms it, just as we critics do, into something he can understand: in his case, a fish. Even in his less extreme moods later in the novel Vardaman continues to act out the readers' dilemma. When Jewel suddenly reappears after having run away, Vardaman has to absorb the mysteries of the corpse, the smell, the buzzards, Cash's broken leg, Jewel's disappearance, Jewel's unexpected return, and the surprise that when Jewel returns and quietly sits in the wagon he and the other Bundrens show no emotion, act as if nothing had happened: "'Here's a hill,' pa says. 'I reckon you'll have to get out and walk'" (199). From that sentence, rendered by Darl, whose repressed hatred of Jewel it masks, we turn abruptly to Vardaman, who is less able to disguise his confusion but no more able to resolve it:

> Darl and Jewel and Dewey Dell and I are walking up the hill, behind the wagon. Jewel came back. He came up the road and got into the wagon. He was walking. Jewel hasn't got a horse anymore. Jewel is my brother. Cash is my brother. Cash has a broken leg. We fixed Cash's leg so it doesn't hurt. Cash is my brother. Jewel is my brother too, but he hasn't got a broken leg.
>
> Now there are five of them, tall in little tall black circles.
>
> "Where do they stay at night, Darl?" I say. "When we stop at night in the barn, where do they stay?" [200]

Bewildered as the readers, Vardaman becomes an observer, nearly helpless to understand the phenomena he observes but nonetheless diligent in reviewing, comparing, and sorting the data and asking the questions in an effort to comprehend.

Exactly what about *As I Lay Dying* is so difficult to understand? Some two dozen details seem naturalizable only by supposing that Faulkner or his characters have simply made mistakes. For example, at one point Cash says that Anse returns the spades he has borrowed to dig Addie's grave while Cash is at Peabody's, whereas later he says Anse returns the spades before taking Cash to Peabody's (230, 248). Most such discrepancies are completely trivial. Others may mean more but probably do not, as when Cash calls the woman with the gramophone "Mrs. Bundren" referring to a time before, presumably, she is Mrs. Bundren (225); or when Addie says that she told Anse she never had living kin, though she has already mentioned and will mention again something her father told her (163, 161, 165), unless we are to presume that she learned his words from someone else. Similarly, while no one can overlook the mysticism in Cash's list of reasons for making the coffin on the bevel, no one seems to have pointed out that even his first three supposedly objective reasons make no sense (77). Such minor discrepancies are likely to abound in a novel that takes as many risks as *As I Lay Dying,* and they are liable to cloud over or blend in with more genuine enigmas.

Does Anse, for example, know about Addie's adultery? Early in the novel, when Jewel in his harsh way shows concern for Addie, Anse somewhat inappropriately—as if jealous—accuses him of having no affection for her. He then comments, "'She was ever one to clean up after herself'" (19), as if he had heard from Addie the same words she uses later in the novel to describe her reaction when Whitfield deserts her. More to the point, Addie makes it hard to see how Anse could not have known, since she says she refused sex with him during and for months after her meetings with Whitfield (167), so that presumably Anse would realize he is not Jewel's father.

Does Anse's knowledge, or the possibility of it, make any difference? Part of the strangeness of *As I Lay Dying* is how often it is impossible to tell what makes a difference. For most of the novel the goal is to bury Addie, but when she finally is buried the event could hardly be more anticlimactic. Cash's allusion to it seems little more than a reference point to set the scene for the fight with Darl: "When we got it filled and covered and drove out the gate and turned into the lane where them fellows was waiting, when they come out and come on him and he jerked back, it was Dewey Dell that was on him before even Jewel could get at him" (227).

Faulkner makes us expect one thing, a burial, and gives us another, a vicious family fight, its viciousness made all the more startling because it comes by surprise in place of and in travesty of something else.

To point out such seemingly capricious narrative selection—capricious because Faulkner could easily have given us the brawl without withholding the burial—is to point out the radically manipulative premise of *As I Lay Dying*. Faulkner's sleight of hand requires so extreme a suspension of the readers' skepticism, so extreme an adjustment in conventional literary competence, that the narrative jugglery seems to take on its own momentum and disguise that it is jugglery, that any section might instead have been narrated very differently by some other character or characters, or might have been narrated by the same character from the perspective of a different degree or mix of immediacy and hindsight.

The differences from earlier works with multiple points of view are in both kind and number. On the quantitative side, the sheer proliferation and pace of change from one perspective to another distinguishes *As I Lay Dying* from the work of Henry James, or even from the work of James Joyce or from Faulkner's own *The Sound and the Fury*. The nearest analogue is the epistolary novel, but to note their quantitative resemblance is to accent their many differences.

Faulkner makes no pretense that his novel reproduces an actual body of documents, which changes—and nearly abolishes—the rules. The plot never turns on the vagaries of the postal system, on letters delayed, crossed, or intercepted. Characters speak (I say "speak" for convenience, since they speak their words no more than they write them) without motive and turn silent without motive; or perhaps we should say that, unlike in a conventional novel, the author's decision to have characters speak or not speak is unmediated by the pretense that the fictional characters make that decision for themselves, though of course they still may be presumed to have motives for the particular things they say when Faulkner decides to have them say anything at all. The distinction is important, because most critics of *As I Lay Dying* see everything as psychologically motivated, and a few less traditional, usually somewhat structuralist critics seem to see nothing as motivated. It is a distinction that continues through every contrast we might make between epistolary form and the form of *As I Lay Dying*. For Faulkner to release his characters from certain traditional restraints, therefore, is not to release himself from them but to change the way he works within them, so that, for example, rather than being purely impersonally narrated or authorless, *As I Lay Dying* becomes, as Wayne Booth puts it (mocking Anse?) "omniscience with teeth in it."[14]

Thus, speaking without any particular motive to speak or not to speak, the characters also speak without audience, sometimes seeming to be lost in reverie, other times preoccupied by mere relation of event, but in any case without reason to adjust or color their words to their listeners (except as they are their own listeners). They also have no particular linguistic restrictions. Sometimes they speak in dialect and with mannerisms peculiar to themselves or their milieu; other times they speak some other language, as when Darl compares the coffin to a "cubistic bug" (209), or when Vardaman says of Jewel's horse, "It is as though the dark were resolving him out of his integrity, into an unrelated scattering of components—snuffings and stampings; smells of cooling flesh and ammoniac hair; an illusion of a co-ordinated whole of splotched hide and strong bones" (55).

Just as the characters speak outside the normal bounds of writing, motive, audience, and language, so also are they outside the normal bounds of time, chronology, and even mortality. When Addie speaks her section she is neither alive nor dead, but somehow both. Instead of the familiar human and literary subservience to place and time, Addie and Whitfield—who speaks after her— serve the novel's place and time, its externally calculated sequence of withholding and revealing. On a smaller scale, as Gary Lee Stonum has pointed out, the same sort of manipulation goes on in individual sections.[15] Stonum notes especially how Tull describes the funeral as if it were happening there before him, and then suddenly projects forward into a future from which he can look back on the three days that follow the funeral (86–87), as if he could somehow encompass both the present and the future (or, if we take the future as base, be at once in both the present and the past). And, of course, to complicate the disruptions of sequence, the characters' hindsight from the future, whether Tull's about the funeral or Cash's about the second Mrs. Bundren, is the readers' foresight. Taken together, all these dislocations produce a seeming arbitrariness of narrative motion and momentum. At any time the pace or direction of the novel may stutter, pause, leap, or somersault, changing in mood as it changes in manner.

Such an unfamiliar set of narrative strategies, in combination with a resistance to generic classification—the novel seeming at one moment comic, at another moment tragic, or epic, or grotesque, pathetic or burlesque—leaves its befuddled readers with three general options for naturalization. We can say, as we usually have, that *As I Lay Dying* is really a version of something already familiar, a logical extension of Elizabethan soliloquy or Jamesian point of view, and that in the final analysis it is predominantly comic, epic, burlesque, or whatever. Such comparisons and categories go far toward helping us understand and refine our responses, but not far enough, resorting finally to a sort of critical retreat. They err by defining the strange too much by its similarities to past things and not enough by its differences from them, thus writing a literary history that forfeits the distinctions on which history depends. A few critics retreat in a different direction, claiming that *As I Lay Dying* cannot be naturalized, that it has no meaning and cannot be understood, but simply is.[16] To say that a text simply is, to describe *As I Lay Dying* as Roland Barthes describes the novels of Alain Robbe-Grillet, as pure writing, is just another form of naturalization to another familiar critical (even if anti-critical) category. It is to mistake Faulkner for the aesthete he had earlier tried and failed to be.

To seek some sort of middle ground between these two positions, accepting the impulses behind both of them, can give us a third option. We can recognize a literature's resistance to interpretation without succumbing either to that resistance or to an interpretation that fails to take the resistance sufficiently into account. Here is where the structuralist concepts of naturalization and literary competence[17] can be a tool for literary history. If we acknowledge that the strangeness of a work challenges the adequacy of our literary competence, of those kinds of things that previous experience has led us to believe literature can be, then, instead of giving up and saying that the perplexing work is without meaning, we must expand our competence in light of our new evidence. We must propose not just a new interpretation, but also a new kind of interpretation.

Unfortunately, I have no convenient term for the new kind of interpretation I wish to propose. Perhaps an inconvenient or awkward term is appropriate, though, for—subscribing momentarily to the fallacy of imitative form—a gracefully precise expression may not best describe a way in which something stubbornly resists description. In any case, my term is *bothness,* and I derive it from studying exactly how *As I Lay Dying* resists description.

It resists description by being more than one thing at a time in a way not adequately described by the now almost too familiar concepts of ambiguity, paradox, and tension, without on the other hand meaning so many different things that it becomes what Barthes would call "plural" (his word for writing that he claims means nothing because it means everything). I will take just one example, the previously discussed subject of Anse's love for Addie, and then let the idea be tested by applying it to a variety of problems.

Is it a paradox to say that Anse loves his wife but cannot (or hardly ever can) express his love for her? To Addie it is. To her, his inability to express love, through language or otherwise, proves his inability to love. But, having already concluded that Addie is wrong to think Anse does not love her, I find the predicament of Anse's love neither paradoxical nor ambiguous. We have, demonstrably, and without the blur of ambiguity, two separable characteristics: first, love—which we generally associate with the ability to express love; and second, nevertheless, the inability to express that same love. Two circumstances that we would normally expect to find incompatible exist side by side without the tension we have come to expect between ideas actually or apparently in contradiction, the tension that leads us to call the relation between such ideas ambiguous or paradoxical.

It is exactly this reversal of what we would expect that sets apart *As I Lay Dying* and, in particular, sets apart Anse. Contradictions, real or apparent, are not unusual in literature, but it is unusual to find things that should contradict each other but do not. We would expect a man who loves his wife and cannot communicate his love to her to be, to say the least, troubled. Not Anse. Is he, then, callous? Yes and no. He is callous in that he hardly minds watching Vardaman rave, stealing from Cash, Jewel, and Dewey Dell, crippling Cash, committing Darl to an insane asylum, and dispiriting Addie, or failing to notice that he has dispirited her. But he still loves her and, though she is gone, honors his promise to her through every difficulty. His is a callous love, a strange enough thing in itself, but all the more strange in that he is completely oblivious even to the possibility of any contradiction or tension either in his love or in any other aspect of himself. He never struggles. The only tension connected to Anse is the tension *we* feel at his oppressive imperturbability.

Perhaps nothing could more reveal the depth of his calm than to recall how transformed he is from his literary model, the tormented Roger Chillingworth of *The Scarlet Letter,* whose dilemma strikingly parallels Anse's.[18] Chillingworth's withered vitality erupts—as if for the first time—at the discovery of Hester's adultery and feeds on the effort to discover and be revenged on her partner. By contrast, Anse, virile and dull, either does not notice or does not seem to care that Addie has betrayed him, and he ignores Whitfield. Love, to Anse, is absolutely unproblematic. He does nothing about it or with it except beget children, when his wife lets him do even that. Anse neither loves despite the fact that he is unloving, nor is unloving despite the fact that he loves. Though we would expect the two facts to be related, in Anse they are not. Neither reinforces or opposes the other. Anse simply both loves and is unloving, epitomizing the bothness that makes *As I Lay Dying* so perplexing.

One of the great ambiguities of *The Scarlet Letter* is its various characters' perceptions of the scarlet letter itself and of its possible manifestations. Does the letter Hester wears stand for Adulteress (the novel never actually mentions adultery), or does it stand for Able, or Angel? Is the sign in the sky a meteor, or a heavenly symbol of the good Governor Winthrop's passing into angelhood, or a heavenly acknowledgment of the adulterer Dimmesdale's gesture toward repentance? Is there a mark, perhaps another A, on Dimmesdale's breast? If so, is it branded from without or eroded from within? Or do some of these potential A's merely signify, like mirrors, the credulous imaginations of the people who think they see them? The ambiguity and tension arise in that, though Hawthorne makes us accept all these possibilities as fictional facts, they are nevertheless competing possibilities.

But in *As I Lay Dying* contrary possibilities often do not compete; they fuse. Where Hawthorne suggests several choices and forces us to interpret, Faulkner in *As I Lay Dying* gives both choices and forces us to postpone interpreting. Hawthorne makes us stop and wonder which it is; Faulkner makes us stop and wonder *that* it is.[19]

Thus at every point, whether Addie is conventionally alive or dead, she is in real but unconventional ways both alive and dead. The first thing that Peabody, the official judge of death, thinks when he sees her dying is: "She has been dead these ten days. . . . I can remember how when I was young I believed death to be a phenomenon of the body; now I know it to be merely a function of the mind—and that of the minds of the ones who suffer the bereavement" (42). Nevertheless, after Addie dies, in the Bundrens' eyes she remains alive. Anse keeps referring to her desires in the present tense, so that Samson thinks he refers to Dewey Dell (109). Vardaman keeps opening the window so she can breathe; and later, for the same reason, he drills holes in the coffin, drilling right through into Addie's face. Still later he and Darl put their ears near the coffin to hear her talking. These are not just illusions of madness, though they are that. They are also, in the world of *As I Lay Dying*, compulsory illusions, because we, too, listen to Addie talk after she is dead. For that fact there is no convenient psychological naturalization, as there might be for the actions of Anse, Vardaman, or Darl. Faulkner does not introduce Addie's section by saying, "Three years ago Addie thought the following," or "Before she died she wrote in her diary." He refuses to give us that ease of definition. And, at the same time that he forces such unease upon us, he keeps his characters immune to it. They see no contradiction in the fact that in some strange way Addie is alive to them while she is dead, and dead while she is alive.

Consequently, the perennial problem of how to classify *As I Lay Dying* becomes a non-problem. Most critics naturalize the novel's generic complexity either by saying that if we look closely enough it is not really so complex, or by saying that the complexity makes the novel absurd or meaningless. But we need not decide whether it is a this or a that if we can accept—and the final judgment I admit must be impressionistic—that somehow it manages to be both a this and a that, comic and tragic, grotesque and heroic, epic and burlesque. Thus Cash's ridiculous stoicism can be laughable—"'It's just the bumps,' Cash says. 'It kind of grinds together a little on a bump. It dont bother none'" (186)—without diminishing his misery.[20]

Similarly, Darl is both impossibly clairvoyant and purblind. He sees into other minds and watches events miles away as if they were happening right before him, but he cannot see into what his family means to do to him. And though he sees so much so deeply and clearly, though he is in a sense the sanest Bundren, he is also mad.

Or is he? Some critics have claimed that Darl goes mad too suddenly; others have hunted out evidence suggesting that he was mad all the time, such as the indication, completely cryptic on a first reading, that people have previously urged Anse to have him committed (35–36). That proves people suspect Darl of madness, but it does not prove he is mad. Hindsight, however revealing, cannot reduce the abruptness of Darl's madness. And if he went crazy gradually, Faulkner would sacrifice the shock that forces us to contemplate the nature of madness, the tenuousness of the border between madness and sanity, and the possibility that we, or some of us, or at least Darl, can be *both* mad and sane.

Until Darl's final section, where he raves and laughs wildly on the train, there are possible explanations, short of madness, for his eccentricity.[21] Even his apparent madness on the train might be seen as a normal reaction to being suddenly and violently betrayed by his family. Furthermore, Faulkner adds a special poignancy, for while Darl looks out the train window at his family, they ignore him. He may think they ignore him deliberately, but they appear not even to know he is there—though, without a commenting authorial voice, the evidence that they do *not* notice must be circumstantial. Vardaman, admittedly not the most reliable witness, thinks Darl has already taken the train to Jackson (239–42). Darl describes how his family looks from the train (244), but when Cash describes the same scene at the same time (249) he never mentions Darl or the train. Only because they do not see Darl, it appears, do the other Bundrens complacently munch their bananas, which is perhaps provocation enough, in Faulkner's grim comedy, to drive Darl bananas as he looks at them for the last time.

Between the fire and the fight with Dewey Dell and Jewel, Darl acts perfectly sane, and he is savvy enough to rescue Jewel from a knife fight on the road into town.[22] In fact, Jewel's recklessness on the road and his and Dewey Dell's furious attack on Darl force the question of who is sane and who is mad. Vardaman keeps the question before us, repeating again and again that Darl went crazy, that Darl went to Jackson, even, in his pathetic attempt (like ours) to understand, that *"Jackson is further away than crazy"* (242). Cash also has trouble understanding, and he keeps wondering almost to the last words of the book (223, 226–28, 249–50).[23] "Sometimes I aint so sho," says Cash, "who's got ere a right to say when a man is crazy and when he aint. Sometimes I think it aint none of us pure crazy and aint none of us pure sane until the balance of us talks him that-a-way" (223). Cash wonders whether Darl, and by implication all of us, might not be both sane and insane, and whether we do ourselves violence by insisting we can be only one or the other.

Dewey Dell struggles before another kind of bothness, struggles to interpret or naturalize it even if by abortion. She is still her old single self, but she is also two people. Watching Peabody, she thinks:

> He could do so much for me if he just would. He could do everything for me. It's like everything in the world for me is inside a tub full of guts, so that you wonder how there can be any room in it for anything else very important. He is a big tub of guts and I am a little tub of guts and if there is not any room for anything else important in a big tub of guts, how can it be room in a little tub of guts. But I know it is there because God gave women a sign when something has happened bad.
>
> It's because I am alone. If I could just feel it, it would be different, because I would not be alone. But if I were not alone, everybody would

know it. And he could do so much for me, and then I would not be alone. Then I could be all right alone. [56–57]

Unlike Lena Grove, who embraces contradictions by denying them, Dewey Dell sees her pregnancy as a paradox, as inherently contradictory. She cannot believe she is pregnant, and she does not want to be pregnant; therefore she contrives her state into a contradiction where none is required. In a world where pregnancy, a biological bothness, is treated as an extraordinary condition, especially for an unmarried woman, Dewey Dell desperately wants to regain what she thinks is ordinariness, to be one and uncontradictory. Faced with what she cannot naturalize or understand, she wants, as we critics want, to revise what she perceives back into some more familiar form. But she cannot do it.

Dewey Dell's fears are a smaller version of her mother's much more complicated dilemma. Addie too feels her aloneness transformed by pregnancy (and, in her case, by childbearing), but what she is transformed to, other than several things at once, remains a puzzle. Her monologue is an almost impenetrable tangle of apparently unwitting contradiction.[24] Where Dewey Dell seeks out and meditates over such contradictions for solace, Addie ignores them. Like Anse, and it may be the only thing they have in common, she is what she is not just despite but actually beyond paradox:

And when I knew that I had Cash, I knew that living was terrible and that this was the answer to it. [163]

I knew that it had been, not that my aloneness had to be violated over and over each day, but that it had never been violated until Cash came. [164]

My aloneness had been violated and then made whole again by the violation: time, Anse, love, what you will, outside the circle. [164]

Cash is both inside and outside the circle of Addie's aloneness. Having borne him both reinforces and relieves the terribleness of living, leaves Addie both more alone than before and for the first time not alone. "I was three now" (165), she says after Darl comes. Later, still with only Cash and Darl, she says, "My children were of me alone, of the wild blood boiling along the earth, of me *and* of all that lived; of none *and* of all" (167; emphasis mine). And yet Darl is not of her in the same sense that Cash is, because, after three more children, one by Whitfield and then two more by Anse, she says that "now he [Anse] has three children that are his and not mine" (168), meaning Dewey Dell, Vardaman, and presumably Darl. Somehow, in Addie's mind, as Cash is both within and without her aloneness, Darl is both of her alone and of Anse alone.

After Whitfield deserts her, Addie resigns herself to her life of bothness, but she does not like it. She blames it on language, on the failure of words to signify meaning. When she had Cash, she says, she

> learned that words are no good; that words dont ever fit even what they are trying to say at. When he was born I knew that motherhood was invented by someone who had to have a word for it because the ones that had the children didn't care whether there was a word for it or not. I knew that fear was invented by someone that had never had the fear; pride, who never had the pride. I knew that it had been, not that they [her students] had dirty noses, but that we had had to use one another by words like spiders dangling by their mouths from a beam, swinging and twisting and never touching. [163–64]

Language, to Addie, is singled out as somehow exempt from bothness. She thinks the signified and the signifier never touch. What exactly such "touching" means is for semioticians to debate, though whether it exists is still for each of us to decide. Faulkner can be said to have decided, in the sense that Addie's divorce of signified from signifier does not work.

She claims that words are so empty they become harmless:

> And so when Cora Tull would tell me I was not a true mother, I would think how words go straight up in a thin line, quick and harmless, and how terribly doing goes along the earth, clinging to it, so that after a while the two lines are too far apart for the same person to straddle from one to the other; and that sin and love and fear are just sounds that people who never sinned nor loved nor feared have for what they never had and cannot have until they forget the words. Like Cora, who could never even cook. [165–66]

Addie's rhetoric is almost convincing, especially her comic argument by analogy about Cora's cooking. But by insisting not only that words and deeds are separate but also that they diverge to the point where words are actually harmless, she becomes revealingly defensive, for her problem is that she knows too well that words are not harmless. Cora's accusation hurts. In fact, Addie has learned both to fear the power of words, and to use it to her own purposes: "Then I found that I had Darl. At first I would not believe it. Then I believed that I would kill Anse. It was as though he had tricked me, hidden within a word like within a paper screen and struck me in the back through it. But then I realised that I had been tricked by words older than Anse or love, and that the same word had tricked Anse too. . . . And when Darl was born I asked Anse to promise to take me back to Jefferson when I died" (164–65). Words thus have the power to deceive, which depends on the possibility that they do not always deceive, a possibility Addie implicitly acknowledges when she uses Anse's promise, his word, to accomplish her final wish.

It therefore means much that Whitfield's section, out of chronological sequence, immediately follows Addie's, for Whitfield suggests that words can but need not be empty. Whitfield's sermon at Addie's funeral, as Tull describes it, embodies perfectly the gap between signifier and signified, the emptiness of language that so distresses Addie: "Whitfield begins. His voice is bigger than him. It's like they are not the same. It's like he is one, and his voice is one, swimming on two horses side by side across the ford and coming into the house, the mud-splashed one and the one that never even got wet, triumphant and sad" (86). Whitfield is an unmitigated hypocrite, rendered without the compassion that Hawthorne grants his prototype, Arthur Dimmesdale.[25] But the usual idea that Whitfield's hypocrisy proves Addie right about the discrepancy between word and deed misses the point. Not everyone in *As I Lay Dying* is a hypocrite. Whitfield's duplicity is not mandated; he chooses it. As he decides not to confess, upon learning that Addie has died without revealing their secret, he says that the Lord "will accept the will for the deed, Who knew that when I framed the words of my confession it was to Anse I spoke them, even though he was not there" (171). With such thoughts Whitfield makes a mockery of Addie's idea. He shows that in his case—which is also Addie's—without the word there is no deed, for some deeds are made of words.

Nevertheless, Addie's complaints remind us that, though language may be a component of truth and sincerity, truth and sincerity need not be a component of language. As she distrusts Anse, and as we are forced finally to distrust her, she makes us read the language of the entire book more skeptically. The shock of suddenly finding Addie speak as if both dead and alive, combined with her outrage at the gap between word and deed, reinforces the sense that the characters' language emanates out of no definable time or place. After Addie's section, Darl's words become more suspect; we start to wonder what sort of deeds they are. Anse's platitudes begin to seem yet more ineffectual. But while Addie's section brings a new mystery to the novel's language, it also reveals startling new information with which we begin to unravel other mysteries in the plot and in the characters' psychological motivations. In effect, in Addie's section the status of knowledge in language and in plot are exchanged. A language we had come to think we knew becomes suddenly indefinable, and a plot we had come to think indefinable becomes suddenly known. Clearly, the new uncertainties about language create new uncertainties about plot, the words and the deeds touch and merge. But Addie helps us explain some things in familiar ways, even as she forces other things into the strangeness, the bothness, so nearly beyond explanation. Let us now turn to those gestures toward more familiar forms of explanation.

III. Toward Explanation

Why does Addie marry Anse? Her explanation is savage and obscure:

> In the afternoon when school was out and the last one had left with his little dirty snuffling nose, instead of going home I would go down the hill to the spring where I could be quiet and hate them. It would be quiet there . . .; especially in the early spring, for it was worst then.
>
> I could just remember how my father used to say that the reason for living was to get ready to stay dead a long time. And when I would have to look at them day after day, each with his and her secret and

selfish thought, and blood strange to each other blood and strange to mine, and think that this seemed to be the only way I could get ready to stay dead, I would hate my father for having ever planted me. I would look forward to the times when they faulted, so I could whip them. When the switch fell I could feel it upon my flesh; when it welted and ridged it was my blood that ran, and I would think with each blow of the switch: Now you are aware of me! Now I am something in your secret and selfish life, who have marked your blood with my own for ever and ever.

And so I took Anse. [161–62]

Until Addie's section, the narrative has withheld from us the secret of her past. That secret turns out to be an obsession with secrecy, so that in her section the narrative secrecy converges with a different sort of secrecy that is its psychological equivalent. Like the narrative, Addie associates secrecy with sex. Both, to the desperately alone Addie, seem the consummate way at once to acknowledge someone else and to be acknowledged by someone else, each direction of recognition, she supposes, naturally implying its reciprocation. Such high expectations set her up to be disappointed in Anse, in love and sex, and in the empty words of love and sex as Anse speaks them.

Before Anse she has nothing or no one even to be disappointed in. She goes to the spring, especially in the spring, as if to cultivate her awareness of the unfulfilled need that both springs symbolize. Overcome by that awareness, she relishes whipping her students as a perverse substitute for the sexual contact she cannot otherwise find, a substitute for sharing the secrets she knows must lie hidden within each person, within each child, as they lie hidden within her. Searching for contact, for communion, she feels the switch as if upon her own flesh and knows that at least somehow her students feel her, that by beating them she has earned a place in their secret and selfish obsessions, even as she can find no one to take such a place in hers. We never learn why Addie seems to attract no other men, but she takes Anse in that extremity of desperation, and not in love.

Anse, however, has either no secrets to share or absolutely no interest in sharing them. Joe Christmas and Jewel resent the connection they see women make between love and secrecy, the pitiful secret dishes and notes that Mrs. McEachern and Joanna Burden and Addie leave just for them. Anse does not even resent; he is completely oblivious. As a result, Addie finds him meaningless, like his words. To her, with no positive trait to define his Anseness, he might as well be dead:

> He did not know that he was dead, then. Sometimes I would lie by him in the dark, hearing the land that was now of my blood and flesh, and I would think: Anse: Why Anse. Why are you Anse. I would think about his name until after a while I could see the word as a shape, a vessel, and I would watch him liquefy and flow into it like cold molasses flowing out of the darkness into the vessel, until the jar stood full and motionless: a significant shape profoundly without life like an empty door frame; and then I would find that I had forgotten the name of the jar. I would think: The shape of my body where I used to be a virgin is in the shape of a   and I couldn't think *Anse,* couldn't remember *Anse.* [165]

Addie's desire to know what makes Anse Anse is so incongruous with Anse's indifference that her question does not even merit a question mark. There is no "something secret and selfish" to Anse, though there is plenty of selfishness. Her response is to give up on him.

Vernon Tull, like Addie, is disappointed in marriage, but his response to Cora contrasts sharply with Addie's to Anse. As he crosses the flooded bridge, Tull looks back to the land and reflects on his marriage in images curiously like Addie's:

> When I looked back at my mule it was like he was one of these here spy-glasses and I could look at him standing there and see all the broad land and my house sweated outen it like it was the more the sweat, the broader the land; the more the sweat, the tighter the house because it would take a tight house for Cora, to hold Cora like a jar of milk in the spring: you've got to have a tight jar or you'll need a powerful spring, so if you have a big spring, why then you have the incentive to have tight, wellmade jars, because it is your milk, sour or not, because you would rather have milk that will sour than to have [no?] milk that wont, because you are a man. [132]

Both Addie and Tull speak out of Faulkner's Keats-conscious preoccupation with urns, vessels, vases, and jars as images of perfection, or as a measure of the distance between desired perfection and achieved reality.[26] Of course, Cora is not the disaster to Vernon that Anse is to Addie; still, the difference between Vernon's attitude and Addie's is striking. Where she gives up on her husband, he takes every inadequacy in his wife as cause to adjust and try harder. If God turned it all over to Cora, he figures, "she would make a few changes, no matter how He was running it. And I reckon they would be for man's good. Leastways, we would have to like them. Leastways, we might as well go on and make like we did" (70). Where others give up, be the problem marriage or logging (135–36), Tull adjusts and adapts. If the milk tends to sour, he finds a tighter jar and a more powerful spring.

Addie, by contrast, turns away from her husband to find elsewhere the something secret and selfish—and sexual—she desires. In doing so she fails to contact Anse, but she reaches, makes painfully aware of her, many others besides Whitfield. Her secret act plants a psychological time bomb in her children's minds, needing only the drawn-out process of her death and burial to set it off and to set in motion the novel of which it is both the center and the beginning.

As I Lay Dying abounds in secrets, and though finally it is less a novel of individual secrets than of a larger and more pervasive secrecy, study of the individual secrets that Addie's secret inspires can go far toward making some of the larger mystery, which I have called *bothness,* accessible. Ultimately even particular secrets represent the primal indefinability in every one of us, what Darl—referring to himself in the third person—calls the "ultimate secret place where for an instant Cash and Darl crouch flagrant and unabashed in all the old terror and the old foreboding, alert and secret and without shame" (135). The only way to survive the primal secret, or the illusion that there *is* a primal secret, is to make individual secrets out of it. The result is that sometimes the exact nature of the individual secrets is less important than the impulse to make the secrets in the first place. Initially, therefore, Addie seeks not a particular selfish secret but just *something* secret and selfish—and presumably sexual; Anse, Whitfield, and Jewel are the forms her something happens to take.

In her husband and children the most basic form we can observe of that primal something is their feeling for Addie. Since they find that something or that feeling threatening, their natural response is to objectify it into something easier to manage. Anse makes it a promise, Cash a coffin and a set of tools, Jewel a horse (at least temporarily), and Vardaman a fish. Dewey Dell objectifies it, or postpones objectifying it, by diverting all her attention to her quest for an abortion. "I heard that my mother is dead," she thinks, "I wish I had time to let her die. I wish I had time to wish I had" (114). Darl objectifies it, in the end unsuccessfully, as Jewel, the rival who represents or reminds him of his own rejection and aloneness. Thus Addie's secret, itself kept secret from the readers for two-thirds of the book and from most of the characters throughout the book, begets the other secrets that propel the novel.

More literally, it begets Jewel, who feels its burden. The marvelous story of how Jewel earned his horse shows him working to free himself from his mother by establishing his own secret in which she cannot participate. In defense, she tries to maintain their bond through yet more secrecy; without Anse's knowledge she gets the others to do Jewel's chores, makes him special foods, and sits by him at night while he sleeps. Jewel buys the horse anyway and redirects his oedipal passion by treating the horse as Addie treats him, alternately punishing and pampering it.

But he does not always objectify his mother as the horse. Immediately after the first and perhaps most fervent description of Jewel "down there fooling with that horse" (11), Jewel speaks in his own voice for the only time, addressing his passionate illogic so directly to Addie that it makes his horse obsession seem almost a figment of Darl's jealous imagination:

> If it had just been me when Cash fell off of that church and if it had just been me when pa laid sick with that load of wood fell on him, it would not be happening with every bastard in the county coming in to stare at her because if there is a God what the hell is He for. It would just be me and her on a high hill and me rolling the rocks down the hill at their faces, picking them up and throwing them down the hill faces and teeth and all by God until she was quiet and not that goddamn adze going One lick less. One lick less and we could be quiet. [15]

Here Jewel has no interest in defining his love for Addie or in choosing some other thing on which to displace his feelings. He does not call his love by the usual Faulknerian word for an indefinable obsession, *something,* but he uses another word just as evasive: *it.*[27] If it had just been me, he thinks, then it would just be me and her. He cannot get beyond a simple tautology derived from a son's—or an infant's—selfish erotic wish to have his mother to himself. Still, he never uses the word *love,* for even though Jewel can be infantile, he is also determined to be a tough guy.

The tough guy in Jewel, however, struggles before the probing, sensitive Darl. Darl's threat to Jewel comes not from their competition over Addie, which is no contest. It comes instead from Jewel's resentment that Darl knows how Jewel feels about Addie and flaunts his knowledge. Jewel the tough guy fears that Darl will disclose his tender side—disclose it especially, perhaps, to Jewel himself.

Defeated in the contest for his mother's love, Darl's tenderness has no outlet except a sort of poetic rumination:

"Where's Jewel?" pa says. When I was a boy I first learned how much better water tastes when it has set a while in a cedar bucket. Warmish-cool, with a faint taste like the hot July wind in cedar trees smells. It has to set at least six hours, and be drunk from a gourd. Water should never be drunk from metal.

And at night it is better still. I used to lie on the pallet in the hall, waiting until I could hear them all asleep, so I could get up and go back to the bucket. It would be black, the shelf black, the still surface of the water a round orifice in nothingness, where before I stirred it awake with the dipper I could see maybe a star or two in the bucket, and maybe in the dipper a star or two before I drank. After that I was bigger, older. Then I would wait until they all went to sleep so I could lie with my shirt-tail up, hearing them asleep, feeling myself without touching myself, feeling the cool silence blowing upon my parts and wondering if Cash was yonder in the darkness doing it too, had been doing it perhaps for the last two years before I could have wanted to or could have.

Pa's feet are badly splayed, his toes cramped and bent and warped, with no toenail at all on his little toes, from working so hard in the wet in homemade shoes when he was a boy. Beside his chair his brogans sit. They look as though they had been hacked with a blunt axe out of pig-iron. Vernon has been to town. I have never seen him go to town in overalls. His wife, they say. She taught school too, once.

I fling the dipper dregs to the ground and wipe my mouth on my sleeve. It is going to rain before morning. Maybe before dark. "Down to the barn," I say. "Harnessing the team." [10–11]

Darl's fascinations show themselves not only in his subjects but also in his transitions—or lack of transitions—between subjects: from water in the cedar bucket, to water in the cedar bucket as illicit pleasure, to the more direct illicit pleasure of incipient masturbation, to displaced self-punishment for masturbation by thinking about Anse's deformation, which—since Anse is his father—is also oedipally pleasing, and from his father to—so indirectly that we cannot even know it on a first reading—his mother. (We later learn that Addie, like Cora, used to teach school [161].) He then displaces the thought of his mother by telling Anse that Jewel is harnessing the team, when really he is thinking, as the next sentence and the next two pages indicate, about Jewel "down there fooling with that horse," which he knows is Jewel's mother-substitute. In short, thinking of pleasure and sexuality makes him think of his mother, which hurts, so he redirects his thoughts onto his rival Jewel.

Eleven of Darl's nineteen sections begin with Jewel in the first sentence, and Jewel plays a major role in four or five of the others.[28] "Jewel *is,* so Addie Bundren must be," Darl reasons in his stirring meditation on identity and existence (76). "I dont know what I am," he thinks. "I dont know if I am or not. Jewel knows he is, because he does not know that he does not know whether he is or not." The insecurity impelling Darl's speculation is summarized in his reverie's final sentence, which serves as both coda and gloss: "How often have I lain beneath rain on a strange roof, thinking of home." His confused thoughts about identity he links finally to thoughts about home. By force of pretense Addie has managed to contain the disruption she has sown in the Bundren home; but now that she is about to die, the disruptive emotions that Darl has long watched torment the other Bundrens, himself very much included, will have nothing to hold them in check. Darl does not foresee that he will be sent away, but as he is about to lose his mother he seems to sense that he is about to lose his home, his family, with her.

Darl, in other words, intuits that deceit and repression are potentially explosive. His insight is not necessarily selective; he senses a hidden power in objects and natural phenomena just as he does in people. "It is as though," he says, "upon the shabby, familiar, inert shape of the wagon there lingered somehow, latent yet still immediate, that violence which had slain the mules that drew it not an hour since" (150). Similarly, he describes the flooded river as portentously as something out of *Moby-Dick:* "The yellow surface dimpled monstrously into fading swirls travelling along the surface for an instant, silent, impermanent and profoundly significant, as though just beneath the surface something huge and alive waked for a moment of lazy alertness out of and into light slumber again" (134). But the latent force of things is threatening only as it represents the hidden desires of people, which he discovers in his mother when he sees her furtively trying to help Jewel through his "spell of sleeping": "And that may have been when I first found it out, that Addie Bundren should be hiding anything she did, who had tried to teach us that deceit was such that, in a world where it was, nothing else could be very bad or very important, not even poverty" (123). For Darl, such turns out to be the case; the potential deceit in everything monopolizes his imagination.

That seeking out of the surreptitious distinguishes his nearly mad reveries from Vardaman's more childlike, temporarily crazed delusions. Vardaman, for example, says at one point, "The trees look like chickens when they ruffle out into the cool dust on the hot days" (52). Later Darl describes a similar scene: "The trees, motionless, are ruffled out to the last twig, swollen, increased as though quick with young" (72). For Vardaman the world is animated; for Darl it is pregnant, in every sense, profound, suggestive of more than its immediate self, teeming with Dewey Dells and mothers of Jewel.

Perhaps the extent of Vardaman's distraction indicates that, because Addie loves him less, her death only confirms for him a fear that he has harbored all along unconsciously. But to say so is to cross into the region where we lack sufficient information to continue psychologizing fictional characters as if they were living people. The superficially inconvenient fact, which critics have not acknowledged, is that both Vardaman and Cash are not demonstrably affected by Addie's deceit except as they respond to its effects on Jewel, Darl, and Dewey Dell. Vardaman is disturbed more by his mother's death than by her deceit.

Vardaman releases his immediate fears at the death of his mother in a manner partly sensual and tactile. As Anse nervously rubs his hand, palm and back, against his thigh, Vardaman, faced with death, runs out to feel, to touch *life* (53), running his hand over the horse and savoring its unproblematic vitality. He then translates his sexual shock into a phallic attack with a stick against Peabody's horses, not satisfied until, as if displacing the loss of his sensual relation to his mother, the stick finally breaks. Curiously, at the same time Vardaman uses a stick to wreck a team, Jewel uses one to free a team from wreck (51); just as through much of the book Jewel, not daring to think, furiously accomplishes things, and Vardaman, also not daring to think, desperately tries to undo, destroy things, as when he takes Cash's auger and bores holes into the coffin—and into Addie's face—until the auger breaks as the stick did before.

The effect of Addie's secret on Dewey Dell is difficult to specify, except as it may dispose her to repeat her mother's act and make her own secret. Dewey Dell, as a woman, does not have the sort of oedipal relation to Addie that we have examined in Jewel, Darl, and Vardaman. Incest, however, is no less central to her than it is to them. They battle a suppressed desire for Addie, she for Darl (unless we hold to the rule, which hardly seems applicable, that desire for a sibling displaces desire for a parent).

Darl seems attracted to Dewey Dell, but more passively, less anxiously, than to Addie or than Dewey Dell is to him. His language lingers over her sexuality: "She sets the basket into the wagon and climbs in, her leg coming long from beneath her tightening dress: that lever which moves the world; one of that caliper which measures the length and breadth of life" (97–98). "Squatting, Dewey Dell's wet dress shapes for the dead eyes of three blind men those mammalian ludicrosities which are the horizons and the valleys of the earth" (156). But though he is the only character actually to mention incest (244), he generalizes his sister's sexuality and never seems particularly allured or troubled by it. In the section where he describes Addie's death, where every detail for which we have some other source proves accurate, he envisions Dewey Dell thinking that if Peabody helped her out of her pregnancy *"then nobody would have to know it except you* [Peabody] *and me and Darl"* (50). Such a thought seems unconsciously either just to leave out Lafe, or to substitute Darl in his place; but because Darl's clairvoyance—when he has it—is so dependable, we should probably consider the thought not his but, as he says, Dewey Dell's.

In her own voice Dewey Dell seems almost to make the same substitution. She would let Peabody, she thinks, "come in between me and Lafe, like Darl came in between me and Lafe" (57). Later, while riding in the wagon, Dewey Dell thinks about incest more directly, and the thought leads her into a daydreaming frenzy of nightmare and terrified recollection of nightmare:[29]

> The land runs out of Darl's eyes; they swim to pinpoints. They begin at my feet and rise along my body to my face, and then my dress is gone: I sit naked on the seat above the unhurrying mules, above the travail. *Suppose I tell him* [Anse] *to turn. He will do what I say. Dont you know he will do what I say?* Once I waked with a black void rushing under me. I could not see. I saw Vardaman rise and go to the window and strike the knife into the fish, the blood gushing, hissing like steam but I could not see. *He'll do as I say. He always does. I can persuade him to anything. You know I can. Suppose I say Turn here.* That was when I died that time. *Suppose I do. We'll go to New Hope. We wont have to go to town.*   I rose and took the knife from the streaming fish still hissing and I killed Darl.
>
> *When I used to sleep with Vardaman I had a nightmare once I thought I was awake but I couldn't see and couldn't feel I couldn't feel the bed under me and I couldn't think what I was I couldn't think of my name I couldn't even think I am a girl I couldn't even think I nor even think I want to wake up nor remember what was opposite to awake so I could do that I knew that something was passing but I couldn't even think of time then all of a sudden I knew that something was it was wind blowing over me it was like the wind came and blew me back from where it was I was not blowing the room and Vardaman*

*asleep and all of them back under me again and going on like a piece
of cool silk dragging across my naked legs*

It blows cool out of the pines, a sad steady sound. . . .

Darl says, "Look, Jewel." But he is not looking at me. He is looking
at the sky. The buzzard is as still as if he were nailed to it. [115–16]

As with Darl and the cedar bucket, we need notice not only the
subjects Dewey Dell addresses but also the links between one subject and another. The progression is dense and tangled but still
partly decipherable. She moves from an incestuous awareness of
Darl, complicated by a sense of oedipal power over Anse, to a
variety of defenses against incestuous thoughts. These defenses begin with a fantasy of killing Darl and thereby violently repudiating
the incest wish. Moreover, to follow the tangle of detail, she seems
to sense the incestuous implications of Vardaman's wild displace-
ment, for she imagines killing Darl with the same knife Vardaman
used on the fish, whose death he has tried to block out as if he can
block out with it his illusion of guilt for his mother's death. Then,
as if she sees through the antagonism of denial by murder, she
turns to denial by indifference, recalling a nightmare of sexless
nothingness that was itself a defense against the incestuous implications of sleeping with Vardaman. The movement from Darl to
Vardaman, from big brother to little brother, defends against her
incest wish by seeming, however falsely, to tame or trivialize it.
Something then woos her out of that contrived neutrality, but the
drift away from it is so imperceptible that at first she cannot even
tell what that something is, until gradually—thinking of Vardaman again—she becomes aware of it as a sort of generalized sen-
suality, letting the wind blow over her as Darl lets it blow over him
with his shirt-tail up at night. Thus, still only half-awakened from
her dream recollection when Darl points out the buzzards to
Jewel, for a moment she thinks he must be pointing out her own
body.

Such delirium is not necessarily typical of Dewey Dell. Even
when some aspect of her love or antipathy is not particularly repressed, her response to Darl can stay calm. Faulkner withholds
the strangest example of that calm only to reveal it right at the
brink of Dewey Dell's literal violence against Darl, so that we see
her capacity for calm almost at the moment when we see her aban-

donment to madness. Vardaman sees Darl start the fire in Gilles-pie's barn and tells his sister, but never tells us, what he saw. He does, however, tantalize us by saying five times that he saw *something*, but that Dewey Dell told him not to tell anybody what (205 twice, 207, 213, 215). We may suspect what he saw, but we cannot anticipate Dewey Dell's real motive in keeping him quiet until we get more information from Cash. At first Cash just says that some-how Gillespie found out (222), and we might then guess how, if we have not already. Soon, however, it develops that Dewey Dell has calmly plotted, not to keep Gillespie from suing or even to keep Darl out of trouble, but to be able to spring the trouble on him in its worst form (sending him to Jackson), by complete sur-prise, and personally. Cash, who reports the scene, cannot under-stand how hate can be calmly built from love:

> But the curiousest thing was Dewey Dell. It surprised me. . . . And then I always kind of had a idea that him and Dewey Dell kind of knowed things betwixt them. If I'd a said it was ere a one of us she liked better than ere a other, I'd a said it was Darl. But when we got it filled and covered and drove out the gate and turned into the lane where them fellows was waiting, when they come out and come on him and he jerked back, it was Dewey Dell that was on him before even Jewel could get at him. And then I believed I knowed how Gilles-pie knowed about how his barn taken fire.
>
> She hadn't said a word, hadn't even looked at him, but when them fellows told him what they wanted and that they had come to get him and he throwed back, she jumped on him like a wild cat so that one of the fellows had to quit and hold her and her scratching and clawing at him like a wild cat, while the other one and pa and Jewel throwed Darl down and held him lying on his back, looking up at me.
>
> "I thought you would have told me," he said. "I never thought you wouldn't have."
>
> "Darl," I said. But he fought again, him and Jewel and the fellow, and the other one holding Dewey Dell and Vardaman yelling and Jewel saying,
>
> "Kill him. Kill the son of a bitch." [226–27]

Perhaps Cash is right not to understand; perhaps Dewey Dell and Jewel respond far out of proportion to the stimulus. But to the limited extent that we can explain their actions, the explosion of

57

violence is proportional to the severity of repression. Darl has come to represent for Dewey Dell and Jewel what they pretend not to know about themselves, be it Jewel's angry love for his mother (revealingly, the same supposed bitch he calls Darl the son of), or Dewey Dell's love for Darl or simply the unavoidable fact of her pregnancy. As a group (excepting Vardaman), the Bundrens seem to exchange repressions. Until their outright brawl they have concentrated on fulfilling Addie's wish and—except partly for Darl, who taunts Jewel—have repressed their fears about each other. By no means has this been an entirely unconscious repression; they have deliberately agreed to postpone sending Darl away (222–23). After they bury Addie and thus conclude or re-repress their anxiety over her, then they can release and attempt to resolve their other anxieties by attacking Darl, by raving incomprehensibly (244), or by remarrying.

Anse thinks getting a new wife can fix his family, can disguise his lack of love for his children, just as getting new teeth can fix his mouth. But the teeth are false, and so is the marriage. As his and the novel's final act, Anse's remarriage is a parody of action, a parody of the comic ending where everyone remarries, a parody especially of the often contrivedly happy endings of Victorian novels, where sometimes the supposedly blissful marriages are only a little more auspicious than Anse's. But whether we call Anse's remarriage a travesty of marriage or a wry salute to it—and perhaps finally it is both—it culminates the novel's developing aura of conclusion. Things are done away with at the end of *As I Lay Dying*. Darl is sent to Jackson, and, watching from the train, he sees about his family "that unmistakeable air of definite and imminent departure" (244). The last three sections all stay in the past tense.[30] Anse remarries, and Cash talks about how nice it is months later to sit and listen to the graphophone, even without Darl. *As I Lay Dying* thus ends with a sense of closure, but it does not end with resolution. By burying Addie the Bundrens put her out of sight—and smell. But we can presume that they only delude themselves about having put her out of mind. For resolution, however unsatisfying, we must turn to *Sanctuary*.

CHAPTER 3

Watching Something Happening Told: *Sanctuary*

Faulkner was made famous by one event in *Sanctuary:* the gangster Popeye's corn-cob rape of Temple Drake. Nowhere in *Sanctuary*, however, is that rape narrated. Though it is the key event of the novel, it is simply skipped over, present only as an absence, a gap. Most critics ignore that gap, while a few cite it as merely another example of Faulkner's assault on readability and sequence. But Faulkner's withholding the rape is no arbitrary frustration of coherence. On the contrary, it is the premise around which the entire novel develops, first as the rape is anticipated, and then as it is returned to again and again. Moreover, the obsession with a single withheld atrocity not only shapes this particular novel; its power as a motivating principle of narrative also redirects the developing Faulknerian oeuvre.

The severity of *Sanctuary*'s central gap is a direct consequence of the novel's elaborate preparation for the incident it leaves out. During Temple's long night at the Old Frenchman place, the novel evolves a rhetoric of half-comprehended, imminent horror, with the protraction of the imminence reinforcing the intensity of the horror. Time after time Temple furiously wails and whirls and runs from the threatening stare of one bootlegger, only to end up somewhere else facing the no less ominous stare of another:

> She scrambled to her feet, her head reverted, and saw them step into the road. . . . Still running her bones turned to water and she fell flat on her face, still running.
>   Without stopping she whirled and sat up, her mouth open upon a

soundless wail behind her lost breath. The man in overalls was still looking at her.[1]

She wailed "Gowan" and turned running, her head reverted, just as a voice spoke beyond the door. . . .

"He cant hear you. What do you want?"

She whirled again and without a break in her stride and still watching the old man, she ran right off the porch and fetched up on hands and knees . . . and saw Popeye watching her from the corner of the house. . . . Still without stopping she scrambled onto the porch and sprang into the kitchen, where a woman sat at a table, a burning cigarette in her hand, watching the door. [42]

She broke free, running. He leaned against the wall and watched her in silhouette run out the back door.

She ran into the kitchen. . . . She whirled and ran out the door and saw Gowan. [49]

"Let her go," Goodwin said. Then she was free. She began to back slowly away. . . . In the hall she whirled and ran. She ran right off the porch, into the weeds, and sped on. She ran to the road and down it for fifty yards in the darkness, then without a break she whirled and ran back to the house and sprang onto the porch and crouched against the door just as someone came up the hall. [63]

When she rose she saw . . . the squatting outline of a man.

For an instant she stood and watched herself run out of her body, out of one slipper. She watched her legs twinkle against the sand, through the flecks of sunlight, for several yards, then whirl and run back and snatch up the slipper and whirl and run again. . . .

She crossed the ruined lawn and sprang onto the porch and ran down the hall. When she reached the back porch she saw a man in the door of the barn, looking toward the house. She crossed the porch in two strides and entered the kitchen, where the woman sat at the table, smoking. [89]

She surged and plunged, grinding the woman's hand against the door jamb until she was free. She sprang from the porch and ran toward the barn and into the hallway and climbed the ladder and scrambled through the trap and to her feet again, running toward the pile of rotting hay.

Then suddenly she ran upside down in a rushing interval; she could see her legs still running in space, and she struck lightly and solidly on her back . . . . [90]

When she recognised him she was half spun, leaping back, then she whirled and ran toward him and sprang down, clutching his arm. Then she saw Goodwin standing in the back door of the house and she whirled and leaped back into the crib and leaned her head around the door, her voice making a thin eeeeeeeeeeeeee sound like bubbles in a bottle. [96]

Temple's frantic running is a gesture of fear thoughtless but thorough, her sense—rightly or wrongly—that she is cornered, trapped. Everywhere she runs, someone is watching her, the men's steady leer seemingly a mere visual preface to the violence that at any moment may follow.

The feeling that any moment may suddenly become, in a perverse or even literal sense, her last moment is reinforced by a series of false alarms. They begin in a terror that soon becomes ludicrous, as Temple hears that "something was moving beyond the wall" and screams wildly, and then we learn that the object of her fear is only Pap, nearly helpless himself (50). But the danger grows increasingly genuine. On her way to the supper table, "Something intervened: a hard forearm," which belongs to Van, Popeye's appropriately named truckdriver, who finally releases her at Lee Goodwin's insistence (62–63). Next time, fresh from bullying Gowan Stevens, Van grabs Temple's coat at the breast and starts to rip it open. Goodwin fights him off, only to have Popeye, with Van lying on the floor at Goodwin's feet, replace Van's hand in Temple's coat with his own, until at Goodwin's repeated insistence Popeye too desists (71–72). Then, however, Goodwin leaves, and through a bloodcurdling scene four times repeated we watch Popeye return to Temple, only, for no reason we can yet understand, to desist again (75, 77–78, 158–60, 208–13).

Against the violence portended by these false alarms, Temple is sometimes given hope or protection by Goodwin, Ruby Lamar (Mrs. Goodwin), or Tommy. But other times they betray her, reemphasizing the precariousness of her position. Ruby taunts and warns Temple: "'Nobody asked you to come out here. I didn't ask you to stay. I told you to go while it was daylight.'" "'Do you

Faulkner and the Novelistic Imagination

know what you've got into now? . . . Do you think you're meeting kids now? kids that give a damn whether you like it or not?'" (52, 56). Having terrified her, Ruby toys with her terror. To Temple's immense relief she offers to get a car so Temple can leave, indicating that, after all the suspense, the violence that had grown to seem Temple's fate will be avoided. A few minutes later, though, when Temple meekly asks for the car, Ruby says—in words the full surprise of which we can appreciate only on a first reading, when we do not already know that Temple never escapes— "'What car? . . . Go on and eat. Nobody's going to hurt you'" (61). Goodwin betrays Temple far more seriously. Though at night he saves her from Van and Popeye, the next morning, when Popeye finds Temple in the crib, Goodwin is about to rape her himself, as we know because he enlists as emissary Temple's erstwhile protector, the feebleminded Tommy, who explains, "'Lee says hit wont hurt you none. All you got to do is lay down'" (96, 97), betraying her trust without even realizing it.

The runs of rhetoric mimicking the wild racings of Temple's fear, the sense that she is trapped, wherever she turns becoming yet again the voyeuristic object of some incipient rapist's stare, the ever more precipitous false alarms, and the unreliability or even treacherousness of her supposed protectors, along with all the more obvious dangers inherent in the plight of an immature seventeen-year-old girl stranded among male criminals (at least two of them murderers) at night in the middle of nowhere with a helplessly drunken escort—any of these things alone would inspire terror, but combined and elaborately drawn out they yield an overwhelmingly ominous suspense, a feeling that at any moment something terrible is going to happen.

Most critics, however, attribute the cause of suspense not only to Temple's foolishness and to the dilemma in which she finds herself, but also to her will. They say, sometimes in more delicate terms, that she wants what she gets. Cleanth Brooks has given what I would have thought a definitive argument against this idea,[2] and though I will add some observations I will not repeat what he says. To believe that Temple wants it is to mitigate the suspense and the terror. Granted, it could be argued that her seeking such horrors is itself the greatest horror of all. But that view

62

seems too abstract, an armchair philosopher's argument that pales beside the naked brutality of its subject.

Temple does not want what she gets. Countless critics cite her poor judgment, her failure to escape or hide, as evidence that really she wants to be raped. But how much judgment can we expect from a childish seventeen year old, who has hardly slept and not eaten in two days and is already in shock as she watches Gowan drive their car straight and unblinking into a tree (38), let alone after the crash and during and after her harrowing ordeal at the Old Frenchman place. Even in shock she thinks to lock her door with a chair, wraps herself in an extra coat, and—just as Goodwin is about to rape her—resourcefully tricks Tommy into defending her instead of helping Goodwin (96–97). Her detractors are right in saying that she also tries to look pretty. She takes off and folds her dress so it will not get wrinkled while she sleeps under two coats and a quilt; she fusses with her hair and primps before the little mirror in her compact. At worst, these gestures represent a narcissistic fool's means of maintaining self-respect in what to her seems a potentially shameful predicament. Temple does not know how *not* to want to look pretty; and by now no critic should credit the still too common notion that for a woman to prefer looking nice when she happens to be among even dangerous men necessarily means she is unconsciously provoking them to rape her. Similarly, when Temple thinks that she wants Popeye to get it over with (212), she does so not—as critics have said—because she wants it, but—as the context can make clear—because she wants to be rid of thinking both about it and about the cruelly protracted expectation that has become just another part of it.

As Brooks suggests, because she has been sheltered, Temple lacks some of the skills that might help her evade harm. She cannot comprehend evil and therefore cannot believe in it. When at last Ruby takes her to a safe place, the barn,

> something rushed invisibly nearby in a scurrying scrabble, a dying whisper of fairy feet. Temple whirled, treading on something that rolled under her foot, and sprang toward the woman.
> "It's just a rat," the woman said, but Temple hurled herself upon

the other, flinging her arms about her, trying to snatch both feet from the floor.

"A rat?" she wailed, "a rat? Open the door! Quick!" [80]

To Temple, the inexpressible sort of horror that Faulkner typically calls "something," so as even briefly to intensify the horror by concealing its cause, is epitomized by nothing more horrible than a rat. Having spent hours on the verge of rape or worse, she now wants to run from safety back to where the would-be rapists await her, not because she wants to be raped but because, compared to the present and specific danger of a rat, the projected and abstract danger of a rape is suddenly unimaginable. The next morning, having survived the threats and the rats, Temple decides the absolute worst must be over: "Now I can stand anything, she thought quietly, with a kind of dull, spent astonishment; I can stand just anything" (87). She thinks she can stand anything only because she has no idea how horrible some things can be. Only moments later she cannot stand even the thought of emptying her bowels without a bathroom, let alone desire or even conceive of the brutal something that still looms before her.

Though Temple neither seeks nor enjoys being raped by Popeye, she is no feminist exemplar: when Red rapes her, she loves it and wants more. To respond critically to Temple's pleading for more is to raise the difficult problems of prescriptive realism, here complicated by Faulkner's use of negative role models. I find that Temple becomes disgusting, and I do not doubt that Faulkner meant her to be so ("her mouth gaped and ugly like that of a dying fish as she writhed her loins against him" [232]), which *Requiem for a Nun* appears to confirm. It seems to me that we must ask whether the good intent in Faulkner's implicit moralizing justifies his portrayal of something so foul, though the question can be asked more easily than we can answer it.

The problem is complicated by Ruby. Ruby identifies men, that is, real men—as opposed to kids and presumably gentlemen—with meanness and harshness (56–57), which she likes, though she has no illusions about life with such men being easy or pleasant. At one point she appears about to leave Goodwin (93–94), but only because he wants Temple, her new rival, not because she rebels against his beating her. Are we somehow inclined to ask less from Ruby (or from Faulkner on Ruby) because she—unlike Temple—is tough and knowing? In her calm amidst violence Ruby is a little less idealized than she generally seems; but at most she is meant to dismay, and not, like Temple, to appall.

In any case, while much has been said by critics and by Temple herself in *Requiem for a Nun* about her supposed love of evil, no one has remarked that for Temple not just any love will do. The evil she loves takes a particular form: coerced sex, be it from Red or later (in *Requiem*) from his brother Pete. It is one thing, however, for an unappealing character to be obsessed with coercion, and another thing for a novel to be obsessed with it, which latter also implies that to Faulkner—rightly or wrongly—the novel's obsession mirrors the readers' interests. Most critics forget that Temple never, not even in *Requiem,* indicates any liking for Popeye's brutal coercion, but the novel itself is as fascinated with what Popeye does as she is with what Red does. And what Red does, of course, is only Popeye's despairing substitute for what he does (or doesn't do) himself, which thus makes Popeye's brutality yet more the center or origin of interest, just as it is the pivot of plot.

Exactly what is Popeye's crime, then, and why does it so compel attention? We have seen thus far that its fascination, and the fascination of withholding it, are first of all a product of our intense expectation that something terrible will happen—exactly what we do not know, but presumably some form of sexual violence. Here is how the novel describes it at the climactic, or anticlimactic, moment, just after Popeye has shot Tommy:

> He turned and looked at her. He waggled the pistol slightly and put it back in his coat, then he walked toward her. Moving, he made no sound at all; the released door yawned and clapped against the jamb, but it made no sound either; it was as though sound and silence had become inverted. She could hear silence in a thick rustling as he moved toward her through it, thrusting it aside, and she began to say Something is going to happen to me. She was saying it to the old man with the yellow clots for eyes. "Something is happening to me!" she screamed at him, sitting in his chair in the sunlight, his hands crossed on the top of the stick. "I told you it was!" she screamed, voiding the words like hot silent bubbles into the bright silence about them until

he turned his head and the two phlegm-clots above her where she lay tossing and thrashing on the rough, sunny boards. "I told you! I told you all the time!" [99]

In a flourish of narrative coquetry, Faulkner acknowledges the event only by withholding it. At first, even the physical setting and the tone in which Faulkner describes it seem to join in the withholding: "the released door yawned and clapped against the jamb, but it made no sound." Later in the novel these words turn out to be perverse puns, but for now their eery calm belies that at last the long-expected moment has arrived. Yet, at the same time, the calm also intensifies the suspense, for we can hardly help suspecting that it sets up a kind of narrative ambush, a sense of security intended only to make some ensuing horror more shocking. Temple herself reinforces the suspense by explicitly voicing her feeling that "Something is going to happen" to her. The sense grows that this is the moment everything else has been leading up to, first as we realize—Faulkner never actually tells us—that Popeye has killed Tommy, and then as Temple changes from saying (or thinking?) that something is going to happen, to screaming that it is *happening* right then. But she screams to, of all people, Pap, someone from whom her words and all other knowledge of her existence are withheld. And as she screams to this void of an auditor, rather than telling of her horror she attributes some obscure but crucial significance to a fantasy of having told; yet she does so at the very point where the novel's central telling is itself subverted, untold.

On the few occasions when critics have remarked at all on the radical withholding of Temple's rape, they have dismissed it merely as Faulkner's joke on his readers, or else as withheld because too shocking. Though it is too shocking and though it is part of Faulkner's perpetual competition with his readers—his insistence on hinting for them what is to come, only at the end to one-up (or two- or three-up) them—surely it is also much more. Faulkner, like Hawthorne and James, could lavish detail without losing a sense for the situation where detail trivializes. Thus *The Scarlet Letter* is a novel about adultery only after the fact, with the adultery itself never doubted but never described. Nor even at the end do we get any reliable description of Dimmesdale's showily bared breast, potentially so fraught with meaning. Similarly,

James tells no details of Milly Theale's mysterious illness in *The Wings of the Dove;* especially on a first reading, when her sickness is suspect, James's awkward excuses in his preface hardly begin to explain the effect of our ignorance. By the same token "The Figure in the Carpet" would lose its defining mystery if it ended by revealing Hugh Vereker's secret. In all these works and many others the fact of fascination is more important than its object, and made more important still because its object is withheld.

Hence the critic who purports to speak out the details of Kurtz's "unspeakable rites" in *Heart of Darkness*[3] hovers on the verge of missing the point. The goal is not necessarily to *know* what, it is to speculate and wonder what, and from that to speculate also about the conditions of knowing. When Kurtz cries "The horror! The horror!" are we more interested in wondering what would horrify the Europeans, or what would horrify the Africans—or might we grow equally interested in the conditions and consequences of horror itself, along with the compulsion (Marlow's and Conrad's—and Faulkner's) to tell about it, and even to tell about it without ever quite telling it itself? In *Sanctuary* Horace Benbow's heartless sister Narcissa asks Miss Jenny who the District Attorney is, so that she can sabotage her brother's case, and Miss Jenny asks why she wants to know. "'I just wondered,'" Narcissa says. "'Fiddlesticks,'" replies the discerning Miss Jenny. "'You dont wonder. You just do things and then stop until the next time to do something comes around'" (180). Faulkner's strategy of withholding compels us not to read the events as Narcissa does, without wonder.

Furthermore, the impetus to wonder comes not just from withholding per se, but also from the nature of the thing withheld, including its role as object for the rest of the book's obsessive attention. The comparably central and secret fact in *As I Lay Dying* is Jewel's paternity. In *As I Lay Dying* the secret is chronologically antecedent to the narrative middle where it is revealed. In *Sanctuary* it is not chronologically antecedent, for chronology is consistent with narrative, but it is still antecedent in terms of narrative impetus. It is, in other words, the goal of everything before it, the fact that motivates the teller—after the fact—to tell not just what came after but also what came before.

This obsession with a single event as motive for telling a larger story was not as clear in earlier versions of the novel, where chronology and narrative diverged in Conradian fashion, as in *Nostromo*. At first Faulkner opened the novel with Judge Drake entering the courtroom to fetch Temple from the witness stand (now Ch. XXVIII). Then he tried beginning with Temple at school (now Ch. IV), then with Goodwin in jail. He finished that version and sent it to his publisher, who rejected it as unprintable. Then he wrote *As I Lay Dying,* and only after that, when the publisher changed his mind and made a set of galleys, did Faulkner extensively rearrange and revise the galleys into the novel's final form.[4] He also cut passages about Horace's past, especially some tediously unsubtle details about his incestuous feelings for Narcissa, thereby focusing all the more attention on the novel's other and greater shocks, those confronting Temple. Thus in his revisions Faulkner changed the motivating and withheld center of attention from something in the past, as in *As I Lay Dying* (and perhaps, in more elaborate ways, in *The Sound and the Fury*), to something in the middle.

Wherever it occurs, the something, the center withheld to incite our interest, is always a crime, which makes it yet more interesting, and specifically a crime of sex and/or violence, which makes it more interesting still. *Light in August,* though even more obsessed with its characters' pasts, also pivots around a horrible crime skipped over in its middle; *Absalom, Absalom!*, as we shall see, resurrects the past's crime so as to relive it—and re-withhold it—in the middle, forcing into a sort of estranged union the twistings and confusions of chronology and narrative. Instead of focusing attention on one crime, *Absalom* keeps adding new crimes—including the crime of incest that Faulkner mostly cut from *Sanctuary*—and making them competitive, so that each one (the crime, or its motive) newly discovered seems even worse than the one before. *Sanctuary* does not encompass as much. Its center never shifts, as *Absalom*'s does several times, from one crime to another; and even though it has a steady succession of crimes, each turns out to be more a repetition of than an addition to the main crime at the center.

What, then, makes one crime sufficient for so much attention (if it is sufficient)? Its fascination seems related to a combination of several lurid appeals, as if the whole grows greater than the sum of its parts; for the one scene collapses several different crimes. At first we know of only two, murder and rape, but later we learn that even the rape has been more brutal than we knew. To see the role such horrors play in *Sanctuary* it may help to look at the remarkably similar role they play in "Berenice," a bizarre story by Faulkner's southern predecessor in detection and Gothic horror, Edgar Allan Poe.

Poe's narrator, Egaeus, has a diseased tendency to block out the rest of the world and withdraw into absolute preoccupation with objects that, he insists, "were *invariably frivolous,* although assuming, through the medium of my distempered vision, a refracted and unreal importance."[5] He lives with his cousin, Berenice, who is given to cataleptic fits, and who is wasting away from some unspecified sickness. Egaeus has shown no interest in women, but then—in what he calls an "evil moment"—he proposes to Berenice, and the story reaches its grisly climax just as their wedding approaches. In rapid succession Egaeus goes into a trance with Berenice's teeth as his sole object of contemplation; then he is told she has died; then, after she is buried, he awakes from a further trance with no memory of the hours since her burial but with an overwhelming sense of horror. It quickly ensues that a piercing scream has awakened the household, that Berenice has been found alive and "disfigured" in a violated grave, that Egaeus's clothes are muddy, and that he has a spade. Finally a small box slips from his hands and "there rolled out some instruments of dental surgery, intermingled with thirty-two small, white and ivory-looking substances that were scattered to and fro about the floor."

The connections between "Berenice" and *Sanctuary* are manifold. Egaeus, or perhaps we should say the narrative he happens to tell, compulsively represses or withholds its horror, which only increases our shock when finally the horror is revealed. *Sanctuary* too skips over its central horror. The difference is that *Sanctuary* tricks us, makes us think we know all the horror it has withheld— rape—until later we learn about the corn-cob and discover that, as in "Berenice," the delay augments the shock.

In neither work is the strategy of withholding a merely arbitrary principle of storytelling that might create the same effect whatever the horror withheld. On the contrary, the two tales concentrate their withholding on a specific horror, on hideous sexual brutality by impotent men. To Egaeus, who can confess his desire only when he sees Berenice about to die, her mouth and teeth are the *vagina dentata* that threatens, if tried, to confirm his incapacity:[6] "The teeth!—the teeth!—. . . with the pale lips writhing about them. . . . I shuddered as I assigned to them in imagination a sensitive and sentient power." As his marriage approaches, Egaeus's desperate fascination with trivia is no longer adequate to repress his fear of sex; he must destroy the sexual object itself. To do that, however, would be to confess his fear, and so he destroys a substitute for the real object; but even that gets so close to the truth that it must be repressed and forgotten. The situation is similar to that often found in Hawthorne's tales, where the plot is precipitated as a young man's fear of sex is made suddenly determinant by his new or imminent marriage ("Young Goodman Brown," "Wakefield," "The Minister's Black Veil," "The Birthmark"). But the defenses of Hawthorne's seemingly impotent men are eerily metaphysical, whereas in "Berenice" and *Sanctuary* the impotent men turn to an almost incomprehensible brutality, as if to place themselves outside desire, in some realm where they cannot be hurt by impotence in its largest sense, the incapacity to love, which in Popeye and many of Hawthorne's characters represents not just a physical or psychical but also a moral failure.[7]

Sanctuary is thus a kind of "Berenice" writ large, less spare and more interpretable, where Poe's methods find more range. Like Poe, Faulkner relies on the centrality of a single prurient gap; and in *Sanctuary* he repeats the gaps in smaller ways throughout the novel. Horace Benbow watches Ruby cut Pap's food and pour sorghum over it. "Then," Faulkner says, "Benbow quit looking" (12). Gowan passes out between sentences, with the narrative skipping over what he cannot remember (33–34); and also between sentences Temple completes the emptying of her bowels that has been too frightening for her to think possible (89). Popeye kills Red between chapters (234–35), and we are never told what he then does with Temple. When the trial ends Faulkner says,

"The jury was out eight minutes. When Horace left the courthouse it was getting toward dusk" (284), making Horace's pain more palpable by leaving the verdict unspoken. That night Horace gets caught among the lynch mob as they decide to do to him what they have done to Goodwin. The chapter ends without telling how or even whether he escapes (289); we know only that in the next chapter, three days later, he is still alive and seems unharmed. As in "Berenice," such gaps relate intimately to the novel's lurid preoccupations, if only because of the readers' prurient curiosity that the withholding sustains by refusing to satisfy.[8]

Hence when Faulkner set out (as later he was fond of confessing he had done) to write a potboiler, he chose two subjects of popular appeal, two ways, in effect, to boil the pot: smut and mystery. It is a curious, even if not unique, combination, implying that Faulkner and/or his presumed audience sees some special link between, on the one hand, women—who tend to be the objects of smut, which (at least then) was written and read mainly by men—and, on the other hand, things forbidden, mystery.[9] Thus to accept *Sanctuary* as deserving serious attention is to acknowledge, with whatever repugnance, the interest of its brutal and sensational subject. Irving Howe, in fact, argues eloquently for the novel's inherent shock value.[10] We have seen, however, that *Sanctuary* depends not just on shock itself but also on particular kinds of shock, violent rape and murder. Yet Faulkner himself seems to condemn our interest in such subjects, for he implicitly condemns the interest of Jefferson's outraged citizens, whose remarks expose the crass lust and amusement within their outrage: "'She was some baby. Jeez. I wouldn't have used no cob'"; "'Served him right. . . . We got to protect our girls. Might need them ourselves'" (287, 291). But surely, even if at some higher level than the characters who make such comments, Faulkner too participates in the lurid fascination; it is difficult to imagine that his book's only motives are to make money and condemn evil. Somehow Faulkner, and we his readers, identify with the things we fear and become more willing to indulge in them when they are confined to a seemingly safe arena like literature. We thus become voyeurs of terror.

And *Sanctuary,* as we might expect of a novel about impotent men, is also a novel about voyeurism, about watching. We have already seen how wherever Temple runs, someone seems to be watching her. The novel even begins in voyeurism, with an incomprehensible scene of unprovoked terror, as Popeye simply watches Horace for two hours. Temple is introduced as the incessant object of other people's watching at the university, and when she and Gowan crash into the tree, Popeye and Tommy step out of the bushes, watching (28–29, 38). Tommy watches Temple innocently, with no sense of the terror his peeping provokes. In her presence he says to Gowan: "'She's a right tall gal, too . . . [with] them skinny legs of hern. How much she weigh?'" (40), as if Temple had no capacity even to recognize his curiosity, let alone be offended by it. Later Tommy watches through a window while Temple undresses, not wanting to be caught, but with little idea that he is doing anything wrong (66–69). Most of the other watching is both more complex and more complexly motivated. Indeed, the scenes where Temple is almost raped are virtual palimpsests of peeping. Ruby and Tommy and Popeye watch Van and Goodwin watch Temple, and then Ruby watches Tommy watch Popeye watch Temple (71–72, 75, 77–78). When the terrified Temple discovers Goodwin watching her relieve herself, she runs away and screams to Ruby, in what might make an epigraph to the novel, "'He was watching me! . . . He was watching me all the time!'" (89).[11] As the rape finally approaches, Popeye watches Goodwin and Tommy watch Temple; then, when Goodwin sends Tommy as emissary to Temple, she converts him to her guardian and has him watch Goodwin. But Popeye arrives and wants to know what Tommy is doing. "'I was watching him,'" Tommy says, "jerking his head toward" Goodwin. "'Watch him, then,'" Popeye says; and when Tommy obediently turns his head, Popeye shoots him (98; anticipating Popeye's own death, 309), so that he can watch Temple by himself, violently. Later, Minnie watches Popeye watch Clarence Snopes watch Temple through the keyhole; Popeye watches Temple while she sleeps and has his goons watch to make sure she stays at Miss Reba's; and, of course, because Minnie herself peeps through the keyhole, we learn about Popeye—whose very name suggests a voyeur—watching Temple and Red.

The significance of all this voyeurism, aside from its prurient appeal, is the response it provokes. In *Sanctuary* the response to watching is telling. "'You'll have something to tell them now, when you get back. Won't you?'" Ruby says to Temple. Later, as she thinks someone is about to rape her, Temple screams, "'I'll tell my father! . . . I'll tell my father!'" (58, 79). When at last she is raped (or, since Faulkner does not tell till later, when at last she seems to be raped) she screams desperately that she has already told: "'I told you it was! . . . I told you! I told you all the time!'" From then on, the telling of this same rape, while nevertheless keeping it untold, becomes *Sanctuary's* center and obsession, just as *Absalom, Absalom!* withholds and yet repeatedly retells from a different perspective what happened that Christmas Eve when Henry Sutpen met his father in the library and then left home.

First, as a series of prototypes, we get the deceptive telling and retelling of near rapes, one of which is told four times, each time more elaborately (75, 77–78, 158–60, 208–13). Then, after the climactic first version of the real rape, where Faulkner works up to the event but skips over it, the two other major tellings of Temple's ordeal are in her own words. Both, however, repeat the original version by yet again withholding the main event, first when Temple retells her story to Horace in Memphis, and again when she testifies in court. With so much obsessive telling about so much watching, all designed to provoke a degree of interest that can survive so much delay, we as readers become not only voyeurs of terror but also, more than for other novels, voyeurs of telling itself, especially as that telling sustains itself by not telling what we most want to hear. Thus the novel is built, like *Absalom, Absalom!,* around three versions of the same tale, one in the Old Frenchman place, one in Memphis, and one in court, with each version elaborately anticipated but with the first two inadequate, creating the need for a second version and then for a third.

In Memphis the earlier rather arbitrary emphasis on telling begins to take on special significance: "'Dont think I'm afraid to tell,' Temple said. 'I'll tell it anywhere. Dont think I'm afraid'" (207). Temple tells her story to Horace in some of the most highly charged writing in Faulkner's novels. Her defensive fantasies of desexualizing herself recall Dewey Dell's reverie in *As I Lay Dying;*

and her fantasy of becoming a man—because of what we might call her unforgettably rendered consciousness of how it feels to have genitals—recalls Addie's thoughts about having been changed by sex with Anse.[12] Horace recognizes with revulsion that Temple's telling about what should be too horrible to tell becomes a spectacle, an exalting of the art of storytelling itself: "Suddenly Horace realised that she was recounting the experience with actual pride, a sort of naive and impersonal vanity, as though she were making it up, looking from him to Miss Reba with quick, darting glances like a dog driving two cattle along a lane" (209). Despite Horace's revulsion, Temple's pride is finally Faulkner's pride, for it is he who is "making it up." Hence we can see a further motive for the novel's proliferation of withholding: such disordering forces the novelist away from mere relation of incident and gives him rein, in effect, to show off.

But at the same time, Horace's loathing, his terrified glance into horror made medium of literary thrill, is Faulkner's also. For once Horace hears Temple's story (that is, once the second major telling is complete) the novel reaches what, after the withheld rape scene, might be called its second climax, this one not so much of horror as of revulsion at the earlier horror. With an apocalyptic sense of impending crisis, Horace returns home sick with the thought of Temple's plight. He stares at a photograph of Little Belle, his step-daughter, contemplating its aura "of invitation and voluptuous promise and secret affirmation."

> Then he knew what the sensation in his stomach meant. He put the photograph down hurriedly and went to the bathroom. He opened the door running and fumbled at the light. But he had not time to find it and he gave over and plunged forward and struck the lavatory and leaned upon his braced arms while the shucks set up a terrific uproar beneath her thighs. Lying with her head lifted slightly, her chin depressed like a figure lifted down from a crucifix, she watched something black and furious go roaring out of her pale body. She was bound naked on her back on a flat car moving at speed through a black tunnel, the blackness streaming in rigid threads overhead, a roar of iron wheels in her ears. The car shot bodily from the tunnel in a long upward slant, the darkness overhead now shredded with parallel attenuations of living fire, toward a crescendo like a held breath, an

interval in which she would swing faintly and lazily in nothingness filled with pale, myriad points of light. Far beneath her she could hear the faint, furious uproar of the shucks. [216]

In a rhetorical orgasm like the "Nausicaa" chapter of *Ulysses,* Horace's fantasy blends Little Belle with Temple and couples brutality with desire, thus signaling his attraction to what has been done to Temple, its bound, helpless victim. That attraction reminds us of his similarities to Popeye. From the beginning they are antagonists, but their reflections merge in the spring across which they are opposed, and Horace's more noble impotence is hardly less crippling than Popeye's.[13] Furthermore, Horace's link to Popeye and his mixture of attraction with revulsion also signal Faulkner's own involvement, through Horace, in Popeye and Popeye's crime. In fact, the relation of the novel to certain aspects of Faulkner's life suggests that *Sanctuary* is partly the vicarious representation—and perhaps exorcism—of Faulkner's own will to abuse and his despair at feeling abused himself, of Faulkner as victim and victimizer.

His connection to Popeye, because more repugnant, is more repressed than his connection to Horace. Popeye has a "faintly aquiline" nose, a "delicate hooked profile" (5, 225) exactly like his creator, though also like many other Faulkner characters. Faulkner used to identify himself jokingly with the act that made Popeye famous. Asked which character he was in *Sanctuary,* he said he was the corn-cob; he told his editor, "I'll always be known as the corn-cob man!"[14] Another link between Faulkner and Popeye relates to Faulkner's anxieties about his wife, Estelle, on whom Temple seems partly modeled—though only partly, for there were other, more important models.[15] Estelle had as many dates and went to as many dances at the University of Mississippi as did Temple (though Estelle's were chaperoned), and when Faulkner could not join the dances he would stand outside, watching through the windows, just as the town boys watch Temple (29).[16] Temple's characteristic comment is her repeated warning that her father is a judge. Estelle's father was not a judge, but she came from a family of judges, and as Faulkner began *Sanctuary,* while planning to marry her, she was divorcing a judge, and there was talk in the papers about running her father to be a judge.[17] For Faulkner thus to make Popeye violate a version of Estelle seems both a jealous slap at her first husband and partly a wish to violate her himself, however much his desire, like Horace's, is mixed with disgust.

Such comparisons are highly tenuous, for Faulkner sublimates his role as Popeye—by which I do not mean he was sick, since we all have something to sublimate—in his role as Horace, to whom his similarities are more direct. Though he had written about Horace in *Flags in the Dust* years before he knew he would get a second chance to marry Estelle, as Faulkner worked on *Sanctuary* he would have had to see the parallels between Horace's dismal marriage to Belle Mitchell and his own prospective marriage, which, if it was not definitely planned when he began the novel in January 1929, certainly was planned before he finished drafting it. He even seems to have conceived it partly to earn money to afford the marriage.[18] Horace's wife has brought a child from her previous marriage, the Little Belle about whom Horace worries and quasi-incestuously fantasizes. Estelle was to bring two children from her previous marriage, the older a daughter, and though Faulkner seems to have been comfortable with his stepchildren, even his circumspect biographer acknowledges the uneasiness that their new stepfather, whose vagabond life they and their mother would thoroughly change, must have anticipated.[19]

Such ideas found their way explicitly into the novel. The always authoritative Miss Jenny complains to Horace, "'It took you a long time to learn that if a woman dont make a very good wife for one man, she aint likely to for another, didn't it?'" (104). In revising the manuscript immediately before his marriage, Faulkner might be expected—for the sake of not offending Estelle, who read it fresh from the typewriter—to have cut such a passage. Or he could have cut it in revising the galleys a year and a half later. Instead of cutting, however, he *added* to the galleys yet harsher thoughts of the same sort, this time in Horace's own words: "'When you marry your own wife you start out from scratch . . . maybe scratching. When you marry somebody else's wife, you start off maybe ten years behind, from somebody else's scratch and

76

scratching'" (16).[20] "Maybe ten years," Horace says; Estelle had married her first husband eleven years before she married Faulkner. Toward the novel's end, much is made of June 20, the date on which Goodwin's trial, where Temple betrays him, begins (257, 261). Two or three weeks at most after Faulkner finished the first version of the novel, he and Estelle were married—on June 20. Faulkner even seems to have dated the trial on the June 20 of 1929, the same year as his marriage, and then to have tried to change the year to 1930 when he revised the galleys. Perhaps that change was a coverup; more likely it was another instance of his general preference for dating novels in the year when he wrote or revised them. Either way he seems, consciously or not, at the time of writing to have identified this grimmest of his books with his own marriage, whether or not he chose first the date of the marriage or the date of the trial.[21] The implication is not primarily that, in his portraits of Temple Drake and Belle Benbow, Faulkner took literary revenge on Estelle for marrying another man— whom she didn't love—when she had promised to marry him, or that once he finally was able to marry her he expected their marriage to fail, or even that it did fail; though all those things may be true, and Estelle even tried to drown herself on their honeymoon.[22] The major import of such comparisons is simply to demonstrate how closely Faulkner involved himself with Horace, the poet manqué who writes "neatly and illegibly" (253) exactly as Faulkner himself wrote, and hence with Horace's enemy and alter ego Popeye, and through both of them with the novel's horror and with its revulsion at its own horror, as those two feelings are violently yoked in Horace's orgasmic fantasy.

Horace reacts to his fantasy by vomiting. It is, *Sanctuary* seems to suggest, the proper response to sex made into brutality, or in any other way made terrorful. The outraged Memphis reviewer who called *Sanctuary* the most putrid story ever written seems not to have been far off in complaining that it "leaves one with the impression of having been vomited bodily from the sensual cruelty of its pages."[23] Temple remembers talking about sex and boys with the girls in her dorm, and how under pressure the ugliest girl claimed to have really done it; "That was when the youngest one turned and ran out of the room. She locked herself in the bath and they could hear her being sick" (147–48). Like Horace, the youngest girl vomits not from the act but from the telling.

As we have seen, however, the telling Horace vomits at is a sort of untelling, for it never gets to the main event. Critics seem to assume that Faulkner simply skips over Temple's telling Horace about the corn-cob, but we can discern that she never tells, because Miss Reba is with them all the time and she does not know. She says to Horace after they leave Temple, "'There's something funny about it that I aint found out about yet'" (213), just as, before he knew about Temple at all, Horace had said to Ruby, "'There's something about this that I dont know yet; that you and Lee haven't told me. Something he just warned you not to tell me'" (128). Already we have seen Popeye enter Temple's room at Miss Reba's, presumably to rape her again, but instead merely staring at her, his face twitching and jerking and his lips "making a high whinnying sound like a horse" (154–55). Gradually we may begin to suspect that the narrative's withholding the something Temple screamed was happening to her has kept from us more than we supposed.

The mystery begins to unravel when Temple finds Popeye's gun (218). Not realizing he has another, she feels safe to tell him what she thinks about him and Red.[24]

> "He's a better man than you are!" Temple said shrilly. "You're not even a man! He knows it. Who does know it if he dont?" The car was in motion. She began to shriek at him. "You, a man, a bold bad man when you cant even—When you had to bring a real man in to—And you hanging over the bed, moaning and slobbering like a—You couldn't fool me but once, could you? No wonder I bled and bluh—" his hand came over her mouth. . . . [224]

> "Dont you wish you were Red? Dont you? Dont you wish you could do what he can do? Dont you wish he was the one watching us instead of you?" [225–26]

The horror magnifies as we realize that not even Temple knew about the corn-cob, that she thought that is what men are like. But hindsight makes it easy to overestimate the clarity of Temple's frenzied remarks, not only about the corn-cob, which has still never been mentioned, but even about Popeye's voyeurism and Red. Soon some of that uncertainty disappears, for Miss Reba, who still knows nothing about the corn-cob, explains about the voyeurism to her friends Miss Myrtle and Miss Lorraine, while Miss Myrtle's five- or six-year-old charge, Uncle Bud, snitches their beer:

> "First I knowed was when Minnie told me there was something funny going on," Miss Reba said. "How he wasn't here hardly at all, gone about every other night, and that when he was here, there wasn't no signs at all the next morning when she cleaned up. . . ."
>
> "Maybe he went off and got fixed up with one of these glands, these monkey glands, and it quit on him," Miss Myrtle said.
>
> "Then one morning he come in with Red and took him up there. They stayed about an hour and left, and Popeye didn't show up again until next morning. Then him and Red come back and stayed up there about an hour. When they left, Minnie come and told me what was going on, so next day I waited for them. I called him in here and I says . . . 'I been running a house for thirty years, but this is the first time I ever had anything like this going on in it. If you want to turn a stud into your girl' I says 'go somewhere else to do it. I aint going to have my house turned into no French joint.'"
>
> "The son of a bitch," Miss Lorraine said.
>
> "He'd ought to've had sense enough to got a old ugly man," Miss Myrtle said. "Tempting us poor girls like that."
>
> "Men always expects us to resist temptation," Miss Lorraine said. She was sitting upright like a school teacher. "The lousy son of a bitch."
>
> "Except what they offers themselves," Miss Reba said. . . . "Yes, sir, Minnie said the two of them would be nekkid as two snakes, and Popeye hanging over the foot of the bed without even his hat off, making a kind of whinnying sound." [250–51]

The murder and rape were made more shocking by the eery silence that made them seem impossible; that same silence—because of our familiarity with the convention of calms before storms—made the murder and rape seem yet more imminent. Likewise, Faulkner's humor, with its contemptuous hint that really the women envy Temple, both mitigates and reinforces the shock of what Miss Reba calls Popeye's "peep-show" (248). Then, as if to suggest the appropriate response, the chapter ends suddenly as the now drunk

Uncle Bud reappears with a slobbering grin that quickly gives way to vomit.

Miss Reba's story reveals that Faulkner has used our presumption of Popeye's normalcy as a detective-novel-style snare to keep us from suspecting the secrets he has kept the novel from telling. Learning that Popeye is impotent thus changes the novel by changing the goal of its detective-style narrative. To the questions of whether Temple can escape and whether Horace can save Goodwin, we find added another question at the barest level of detection, namely, What happened? Exactly what—we find ourselves shuddering to ask—did Popeye do to Temple, and how did he do it? First came the elaborate, suspenseful telling about what happened at the Old Frenchman place, which worked up to the point only to skip over it. Then, with the crimes committed, came the detective or investigative drama, with Horace trying to discover the evidence that he needs to acquit Goodwin. That second movement of narrative culminates in another telling, Temple's telling to Horace, which, instead of skipping over the point, never even reaches it. Then we learn that because Popeye is impotent, the point, the something, that before had been skipped over or simply evaded could not have been what all along we had glibly assumed it to be. Thus the new discovery about Popeye creates yet a further gap superimposed upon the gap that has by now become familiar, with the new gap increasing the need for a new telling, the third major movement of narrative, this time one where telling is compelled: the trial.

Immediately as the trial begins, however, Horace senses that it will be a mis-telling. He sees the Memphis "Jew lawyer" and merely from that, without even seeing Temple, he knows his case is lost. At that moment the galley version interpolates a sudden recollection of Horace's that tersely summarizes his revulsion, but that Faulkner later cut, perhaps because it was too closely connected to the corn-cob brutality about which Horace does not yet know:

> Once when he was a boy he had two possums in a barrel. A negro told him to put a cat in with them if he wanted to see something, and he had done so. When he could move at all he ran to his mother in a

passion of crying that sent him staggering and vomiting toward the house. All that night he lay beneath an ice-pack in a lighted room, tearing himself now and then by main strength out of a writhing coil of cat-entrails, toward the thin, shawled figure of his mother sitting beside the bed.[25]

Horace's memory mimics the larger form of the narrative as a whole, with its temporarily withheld something, around which the incident revolves, that turns out to be horribly brutal, and to which the only proper response is nausea. Likewise, the trial, where under the pressure of oath we would expect witnesses to tell all, nevertheless continues that same pattern of telling a mysterious something instead of the something that happened. But this time the telling has two contrasting audiences, whereby the telling of one thing to one audience—the jury and townspeople, is the telling of something quite different to another audience—the lawyers, the defendant and his wife, the readers.

Temple lies. We are left to speculate why, though there seems no alternative to the explanation put forward by Cleanth Brooks that Popeye compels her testimony, with Eustace Grimm's cooperation.[26] Yet *something* seems to go on in the courtroom that no critic has remarked:

She sat in an attitude at once detached and cringing, her face fixed on something at the back of the room. . . .

"What is your name?" She did not answer. She moved her head slightly, as though he had obstructed her view, gazing at something in the back of the room. "What is your name?" he repeated, moving also, into the line of her vision again. . . .

Her head moved faintly, as though she would see beyond him. He moved into her line of vision, holding her eyes. . . .

"You were in hiding, then, because something had happened to you and you dared not—"

. . . Temple's head had moved again. The District Attorney caught her gaze and held it. . . .

The District Attorney stepped aside. At once the girl's gaze went to the back of the room and became fixed there. The District Attorney returned, stepped into her line of vision. She moved her head; he caught her gaze and held it. . . .

"Your Honor and gentlemen, . . . I shall no longer subject this ruined, defenseless child to the agony of—" he ceased; the heads turned as one and watched a man come stalking up the aisle toward the Bench. He walked steadily, paced and followed by a slow gaping of the small white faces, a slow hissing of collars. . . . He passed the witness stand without a glance at the witness, who still gazed at something in the back of the room, walking right through her line of vision like a runner crossing a tape, and stopped before the bar. . . .

The old man turned slowly. . . . Behind him the witness had not moved. She sat in her attitude of childish immobility, gazing like a drugged person above the faces, toward the rear of the room. The old man turned to her and extended his hand. She did not move. . . . The old man touched her arm. She turned her head toward him. . . .

Half way down the aisle the girl stopped again . . ., then she moved on. . . . Again the girl stopped. She began to cringe back, her body arching slowly, her arm tautening in the old man's grasp. He bent toward her, speaking; she moved again, in that shrinking and rapt abasement. Four younger men were standing stiffly erect near the exit. . . . Then they moved and surrounded the other two, and in a close body, the girl hidden among them, they moved toward the door. Here they stopped again; the girl could be seen shrunk against the wall just inside the door, her body arched again. She appeared to be clinging there, then the five bodies hid her again and again in a close body the group passed through the door and disappeared. [277–82]

There is no way to prove that Temple is looking at anything, but she seems to be looking at something. It cannot be her father, because of the way he crosses her line of sight without disturbing her. It cannot plausibly be her four brothers, for Temple has been so obsessed with her father ("My father's a judge") that it is hard to believe they would attract her eye more than he does, especially when he enters the courtroom so dramatically that hers are the only eyes not on him. And as she leaves she still wants to look at something other than her brothers or her father or even the Memphis lawyer who presumably works for Popeye. It seems that either Popeye is in the courtroom, which is unthinkable, for there are too many people who would recognize him and he is wanted for murdering Red (nor is he the sort to wear a disguise), or he has sent his henchmen, just as he sent them to the Grotto when he went there to kill Red. Through such playfulness about what holds Temple's attention the narrative creates a new and minor something even as, during the same testimony, it divulges the long-kept secret of the major something it has depended on all along: the corn-cob rape.

Yet, in a flourish of withholding that by this point, because it hides nothing, is only a kind of novelist's braggadocio about his ingeniously persistent stubbornness, even the trial never tells what happened. Though the bloody corn-cob is held up in the courtroom and the details of the rape finally grow comprehensible to Horace, Lee and Ruby, and the readers, still the gynecologist's testimony is skipped over, Temple accuses the wrong man, and to maintain a semblance of decorum the District Attorney refrains from actually saying what he suggests happened.

Nevertheless, the implication is clear, and the sudden imposition of clarity changes the novel again, and far more completely than did the earlier changes from one narrative movement to another. Before, the changes were from question to question: First we ask, Can Temple escape? Next, Can Horace save Goodwin? And then, What happened? The trial does away with questions and replaces them with a single answer, the grim answer of the corn-cob: Temple cannot escape, Horace cannot save Goodwin, something happened that is even more outrageous than we thought. By the time we finally discover the object of that outrage, it has been invested with a greater horror by the elaborate buildup and the circumstances—surprise witness and perjury and condemnation of the innocent—under which it is revealed. But this time, now that the withholding ends, the increase of horror does not bring with it an increase of wonder. The absoluteness of the revelation puts a stop to the wonder—except as the shock itself becomes a substitute object for wonder—and therefore finishes the novel with unquestioning resolution, which marks a crucial change from Faulkner's earlier novels. In *As I Lay Dying* the revelation of tactical secrets left uneroded a larger, epistemological secrecy more profound or at least more mysterious than the individual secrets out of which it was built. But *Sanctuary,* through its emulation of the detective novel, confines its mysteries to the nitty-grittiest level. Hence the only meaning of the corn-cob, the revealed object of obsessive withholding, is its radicalness as a symbol of desperate impotence and realized evil.

The sudden change to certainty in *Sanctuary* turns out to be an enabling innovation in Faulkner's continuing experiments with novel form. Having developed mystery around withholding in *The Sound and the Fury* and *As I Lay Dying,* and then having discovered in *Sanctuary* a way in which mystery could be developed only to be the more shockingly demystified at the end, Faulkner was then able to mix modes in his next two major novels. In *Light in August* and *Absalom, Absalom!* he again organizes his narratives around single obsessively withheld violent crimes (the murders of Joanna Burden and Charles Bon), yet in the end he questions—as he does not in *Sanctuary*—what it means to solve (or to think we solve) the mystery. We know only too well what it means to solve the mystery in *Sanctuary.* Where *The Sound and the Fury* and *As I Lay Dying* end with difficulty or defamiliarization (Benjy's and Anse's sorts of order not being our own), *Sanctuary* begins in difficulty and ends with a frightening clarity absolutely antithetical to Faulkner's other novels.

After the imposition of so radical a clarity, the remaining three chapters add little, responding not to the readers' curiosity proper so much as to the remnants of that curiosity, the wish to know what happens to the characters now that the main plot is over. The first of these three chapters follows Horace through his unbelieving despair after the trial. Past midnight a mob burns Goodwin, and, as Horace runs into the throng to see what has happened, a man carrying an oil can explodes into flame:

> Horace ran among them; they were holding him, but he did not know it; they were talking, but he could not hear the voices.
> "It's his lawyer."
> "Here's the man that defended him. That tried to get him clear."
> "Put him in, too. There's enough left to burn a lawyer."
> "Do to the lawyer what we did to him. What he did to her. Only we never used a cob. We made him wish we had used a cob."
> Horace couldn't hear them. He couldn't hear the man who had got burned screaming. He couldn't hear the fire, though it still swirled upward unabated, as though it were living upon itself, and soundless: a voice of fury like in a dream, roaring silently out of a peaceful void. [289]

Here the novel returns yet again to its obsessive subject, for Goodwin's burning reenacts the rape of Temple, as if to remind us that everything not leading toward her rape is driven to repeat it. The implication is that Goodwin has been not only burned but also brutalized—"We made him wish we had used a cob." The repetition of the earlier crimes—murder and violation, with the criminals themselves announcing their acts as repetition—is complete, even to repeating the narrative's withholding of the actual crimes. And the brutalizing of Temple is repeated not only on Goodwin but also—at least in the telling—on Horace. For Horace's trauma further repeats Temple's (99) in his own repression, with him, like Temple before him, suddenly refusing to hear, and in the novel's repression, once again breaking off the incident by ending the chapter and then not returning to complete what was interrupted. When the narrative returns to Horace two days later, in the next chapter, he appears healthy, but we never learn how he escaped, or even whether he escaped unharmed. By that point the defeated Horace has painfully put the recent events behind him. Only then, in the last two chapters, does the novel finally get past its central event. Faulkner's reiterating that event one last time, after the trial has settled what happened, confirms the gradually accruing sense that the obsession with that event is the novel's distinguishing feature, and consequently that anything that might follow, however significant in itself, can be only a kind of aftermath, a coda.

Indeed, the tone of the final two chapters is drastically changed, from the lurid raciness Faulkner himself described by saying he wore out three records of Gershwin's "Rhapsody in Blue" while writing it, to a tone of passivity and despair.[27] As at the end of so many Matthew Arnold poems, the change of mood, in this case reinforced by progressively greater removals in locale—to Kingston, then to Alabama, and then to Paris—is as important as the particular mood changed to. It presages the less grim, even cheerful turn at the end of *Light in August*, which also turns separately to the ends of three separate characters. But the two novels' endings have little else in common. *Light in August* ends with new characters and the promise of new lives for some of the old characters—with resolution, but also with new direction. *Sanctuary*

85

ends merely by adding to its despairing resolution a certain con-
templativeness, a pensive[28] movement dissolving from the cal-
lously narcissistic Temple, pondering her face before the little
mirror in her compact, to that larger but no less dismal world of
which she is oblivious, the world into which her eyes can only
"seem" to follow:

> She closed the compact and from beneath her smart new hat she
> seemed to follow with her eyes the waves of music, to dissolve into the
> dying brasses, across the pool and the opposite semicircle of trees
> where at sombre intervals the dead tranquil queens in stained marble
> mused, and on into the sky lying prone and vanquished in the embrace
> of the season of rain and death.

CHAPTER 4

Something Various:
Light in August

The morning before he razors off most of Joanna Burden's head, Joe Christmas sits down to read a "magazine of that type whose covers bear either pictures of young women in underclothes or pictures of men in the act of shooting one another with pistols,"[1] a stereotypical magazine of stereotypes, through which Faulkner gives us a further stereotype of how fiction and novels are supposed to be read, as he makes Joe read the "magazine straight through as though it were a novel" (104). No one more than Faulkner writes novels that so defy the notion that plot should move in a straight line. Perhaps some other novels, such as *Finnegans Wake,* to name one of the more extreme, are given less to rigid sequence, but no others so thoroughly frustrate an expectation of sequence that they have taken such pains to raise in the first place. And no novel by Faulkner, except perhaps *Absalom, Absalom!,* is more profuse with withholding, with frustrated sequence, than *Light in August.*

Rarely in *Light in August* do more than a few pages go by without some mysterious something, such as the "something," the burden, that motivates Joanna Burden ("I think it was something about father, something that came from the cedar grove to me, through him. A something that I felt that he had put on the cedar grove, and that when I went into it, the grove would put on me so that I would never be able to forget it" [238–40]), or the something, apparently a murder, that Joe Christmas commits on the road to Memphis (50, 74, 92; cf. 81). Almost all the major characters and events are built out of such mysteries. Lena's past is conspicuously unmysterious, but we encounter Joanna Burden,

Gail Hightower, Byron Bunch, Eupheus Hines, and Joe Christmas long before we learn their pasts, and yet we grow familiar with them burdened by a sense that they are somehow the products of those pasts that we do not know. Joe Christmas especially is introduced as a mystery man; we hear about him in Chapter 2 before, in effect, we meet him, in a proletarian version of our rumor-ridden introductions to Ahab or Kurtz or Gatsby. Individually, such withholdings serve mainly to quicken our curiosity; collectively, they define a world and an epistemological vision, a world built enigmatically out of a past that cannot be known but that cannot help being remembered ("Memory believes before knowing remembers . . .," [111]).

Thus in *Light in August* such withholding develops a perspective, a pervasive technique, or even a structure of inverted structure, as opposed to the familiarly linear structure of most novels, and even as opposed to the structure of interrupted linearity in *As I Lay Dying, Sanctuary,* and *Absalom, Absalom!* Having learned the value of interrupted linearity by raising it to a full-scale narrative system in the detective-story strategy of *Sanctuary,* Faulkner retains in *Light in August* the generally detective-story principle of effect before cause. But this time, instead of running the plot through a private eye's sequence of feints, he so proliferates his effects before causes that the aura of detective story becomes itself a feint, the novel's chief false lead. For *Light in August* elaborately gestures toward the detective-story formula and then turns gradually to what we will here come to see as a critique of all formula, be it the formula of racial stereotype or the formula of feminine and masculine stereotype in Joe's magazine. That is, it parodies fiction's formulaic subject, and it also parodies Joe's stereotypical way of reading—straight through; that is, it also parodies fiction's formulaic form.

Nevertheless, at first the gesture in *Light in August* toward a detective-story structure appears genuine. For a while we seem to have another story of crime and murder. As in *As I Lay Dying, Sanctuary,* and *Absalom, Absalom!,* a single withheld event is at the center: Joe Christmas's murder of Joanna Burden, committed between paragraphs (267). Of all events in Faulkner's oeuvre, the withheld murder of Joanna Burden is the one most conspicuously referred to, usually by Joe Christmas himself, as "something," that word that calls our attention to things without revealing what they are. As we approach the murder in Chapter 5, Joe thinks the same thoughts in the same words that Temple Drake speaks in *Sanctuary*:[2] "*Something is going to happen to me. I am going to do something*," and the chapter ends as he thinks again: "*Something is going to happen. Something is going to happen to me*" (97, 110). The next six chapters flash back in time, reviewing the events in Joe's life from age five on that have carried him to this impasse, until Chapter 12 returns to the same evening as Chapter 5, and again Joe thinks: "'I have got to do something. There is something that I am going to do,'" and "'I am going to do something. Going to do something'" (256, 261; see also 76, 77, 84). Then he does it: he kills Joanna Burden.

Or at least we presume he kills her. Few readers recall that the actual murder is itself killed within the narrative, simply skipped right over, and no critic paid attention to that gap until a brief article by Stephen Meats in 1971.[3] Meats reminds us of the abundant circumstantial evidence indicating Joe Brown (Lucas Burch) as the killer. Brown is found at the scene of the crime, tries to prevent the body from being discovered, runs away, lies to the sheriff about when he supposedly discovered the murder, and averts suspicion only when he tells his interrogators that his partner, whom he accuses, is part black, which single characteristic alleged by a habitual liar persuades them that his partner, Joe Christmas, must be the murderer. Presumably, as Byron guesses (93), Christmas killed Joanna, and then Brown discovered the body and, fearful and confused, set the fire to destroy any evidence that might implicate himself. The point is that Faulkner develops an elaborate, detective-story feint to make us suspect Brown, to keep us—for a while at least—less than confident that Christmas did it. Our confusion over the matter permits the moral drama in which the town believes Brown innocent and Christmas guilty merely because of Brown's remarks about Christmas's being part black, merely because of transparently facile formula. And the same confusion forcibly reminds us that the actual murder remains withheld.

What, then, is the overall significance, tactical or epistemological, of that withholding? Curiously, it hasn't the thematic import of the central withholdings in *As I Lay Dying, Sanctuary,* or *Absalom, Absalom!* But in a few broad passings of the novelist's needle, the withheld murder stitches together the separate pieces of the book's beguilingly diverse plot, just as the scene of the crime, the Burden house, is the hub of a set of paths "which radiated from the house like wheelspokes" (243).[4] For the first half of the novel, into Chapter 13, most of the story revolves around or pointedly works up to the murder, which thereby gives the loosely organized material a certain structural coherence, first as the various characters keep looking at the smoke rising ominously in the distance, and later as the narrative traces Joe Christmas's past so as to help us understand his motive for the murder that that smoke symbolizes.

In Chapter 4 especially, where Byron tells Hightower about the murder, Faulkner provokes our interest (and Hightower's) by having Byron tell about it in a coyly staggered succession of withholdings and revelations. After referring to the fire, he begins to hint that there has also been a murder (75) without explicitly saying so. Then he indicates that he is about to reveal some startling fact, but he only reveals part of it, which turns out to be not murder, as we would expect, but instead that "'Christmas is part nigger'" (82–83). Then, having provoked all the more our interest in a possible murder, because of the lurid appeal of anticipated race conflict, Byron draws out his story yet longer, describing not the murder but instead the fire, until at last (85) he reveals the main event—indirectly—by telling how the man who discovered the fire also discovered Joanna's body.

Thus, through Byron, we get the murder after the fact. Immediately in the next chapter we go back in time and see Joe as he is about to kill Joanna, but just when we expect the murder Faulkner gives us instead the long flashback about Joe's past. As in *Sanctuary,* this taunting combination of suggestion coupled to withholding heightens our interest in the thing withheld, just as the continual postponement of contact between the novel's various characters heightens our sensitivity to what such contact might mean—even when it never comes, as between Joe and Lena, whose contact carries a greater weight by being only the inverted contact of frustrated expectation, of conspicuous default. But the absence of any meeting between Joe and Lena, though of much more epistemological significance than the absence of the murder, is withholding of only the loosest kind, since there is in a sense nothing to withhold, it being an absence not only in narrative but also in the plot itself, as opposed to the withholding proper of the murder, present in plot but absent in narrative.

The detective story of withheld murder thus serves a tactical purpose as an organizing principle of narrative, but only for the first half of the novel. Its organizing ominousness, though alluringly suspenseful, utterly lacks the prying compulsion with which *Sanctuary* is organized around a similarly central withheld crime. The difference is that, unlike in *As I Lay Dying, Sanctuary,* or *Absalom, Absalom!,* by the end of *Light in August* we must cast away any suspicion that the particular details of the crime withheld make any difference. There comes finally no dramatic revelation of those details, as in the other novels, and we never get the shock of finding that two-thirds of the way through as in *As I Lay Dying,* or near the end as in *Sanctuary,* or several times as in *Absalom,* we have in an instant drastically to reinterpret everything we have read. In fact, outside Chapter 4, the centrality of the withheld murder in *Light in August* has little to do with its being withheld. The murder is simply the focal incident of plot, the shared shock that twists together at one point a set of strands otherwise kept unentangled. The mystery of its details serves mainly the secondary, non-detective story, only partly tactical purpose of enhancing the already considerable mystery behind its agent, Joe Christmas.

That mystery, carried over from the novel's first half, is one of the major quandaries of its second half: the withholding from readers and characters alike of whether Joe Christmas does or does not have any black blood, a merely finicky withholding that is allied by circumstance to the more fundamental withholding of his motivation. Otherwise, in the second half of the novel the withholding is of a more standard sort: overlapping incident, especially in the capture and murder of Christmas, and secrets about parentage (Christmas's and perhaps Hightower's), either of which is familiar to readers of Dickens or of countless other novelists.

Hence the two most significant withholdings in *Light in August*, taken as a whole, are of the murder itself, the withholding of which—by Faulknerian standards—is but modestly provocative, and of Joe's motivation, including whether or not he actually has that obscure fraction of black blood he is said to have.

Joe's problem is crucial, and genuinely epistemological, though much of the novel, including the Gail Hightower and especially the Byron Bunch and Lena Grove sections, has little to do with it. In the memorable phrase of Alfred Kazin, Joe "is an abstraction seeking to become a human being."[5] Perhaps it would be more accurate to say that he is a human being who cannot quite convince himself he is not the abstraction other people take him to be. Such a judgment is necessarily impressionistic, for we see Joe mainly from the outside, as if to suggest he is all compulsion and no consciousness. Our few glimpses into his thoughts are revealing only enigmatically. One such glimpse comes after he has evaded the men and dogs who hunt him for killing Joanna Burden:

> It is just dawn, daylight: that gray and lonely suspension filled with the peaceful and tentative waking of birds. The air, inbreathed, is like spring water. He breathes deep and slow, feeling with each breath himself diffuse in the neutral grayness, becoming one with loneliness and quiet that has never known fury or despair. "That was all I wanted," he thinks, in a quiet and slow amazement. "That was all, for thirty years. That didn't seem to be a whole lot to ask in thirty years." [13; see also 108]

The "that" Joe wants, the "becoming one," is a bit of a something itself, since by calling it "that" he avoids saying exactly what it is; but it seems fair to connect it with an earlier moment when he thinks roughly the same thing in fewer but more precise words: *"All I wanted was peace"* (104; cf. 263). Joe's desire for peace has a long textual history. Hightower too thinks, "'I just wanted peace'" (293). But *Light in August*, much like Conrad's *Victory* (with its Hightower-like Heyst and its own Lena) seems to suggest that peace is almost impossible. Even though Joanna Burden supplies the town "at last with an emotional barbecue, a Roman holiday almost, they would never forgive her and let her be dead in peace and quiet. Not that. Peace is not that often" (273). Horace

Benbow uses a similar expression in his pitiful last appearance in *Sanctuary*, as he resigns himself to impotence and defeat, looking out a door through which comes a "vague, troubling wind. . . . He began to say something out of a book he had read: 'Less oft is peace. Less oft is peace.'"[6] Horace's unattributed something comes from Shelley's "To Jane: The Recollection," in which a cherished calm is interrupted by an "envious wind," leading the poet to lament in his closing lines that "Less oft is peace in Shelley's mind,/ Than calm in waters, seen." Though *Light in August* as a whole is considerably less grim than *Sanctuary*, Joe's fate is as unrelievedly stark as Horace's. Joe is killed and castrated by grimness personified (Percy Grimm), and he never finds peace, except once, and then so fleetingly that it makes his failure to find it again even more painful.

Joe finds his fleeting peace with his prostitute lover, Bobbie Allen. The full dreariness of his fate as a whole inclines us to forget what seems an uncharacteristic happiness with Bobbie. After he gets over his shock that she menstruates, that as a woman she is distinctively other than men, we see Joe not only content with Bobbie, but even so content that, in a scene of peaceful and intimate physical touch, he trades secrets with her and dares put his happiness to what seems to him the final test:

> She told him about the sickness of the first night. It did not shock him now. Like the nakedness and the physical shape, it was like something which had never happened or existed before. So he told her in turn what he knew to tell. He told about the negro girl in the mill shed on that afternoon three years ago. He told her quietly and peacefully, lying beside her, touching her. Perhaps he could not even have said if she listened or not. Then he said, "You noticed my skin, my hair," waiting for her to answer, his hand slow on her body. . . .
>
> His hand was slow and quiet on her invisible flank. . . . Then he told her. "I got some nigger blood in me."
>
> Then she lay perfectly still, with a different stillness. But he did not seem to notice it. He lay peacefully too, his hand slow up and down her flank. "You're what?" she said.
>
> "I think I got some nigger blood in me." His eyes were closed, his hand slow and unceasing. "I don't know. I believe I have."
>
> She did not move. She said at once: "You're lying."

"All right," he said, not moving, his hand not ceasing.
"I dont believe it," her voice said in the darkness.
"All right," he said, his hand not ceasing. [184–85]

The steady, comfortable movement of Joe's hand against her flank—Faulkner mentions it seven times and twice calls it peaceful—distinguishes this scene from all Joe's other contact with women, and from all the alienated angst that two generations of readers and critics have come to associate with Joe Christmas. The scene looks forward strangely to the novel's other bed scene, also peaceful, in the last chapter of the book, which—when it has not been forgotten—has been seen by readers as antithetical to everything Joe suggests. To be sure, the bed talk at the book's close, between the furniture dealer and his wife, is more comic and more fully peaceful. But even as the bed scene between Joe and Bobbie teeters away from peace and toward the pain of the rest of Joe's life, even as Bobbie changes to a different stillness, translates his I *got* to her you *are,* and says not that it doesn't matter but rather that it isn't so, even as she thus comes so close to hurting him, the scene becomes the more remarkable for stopping short of the pain and staying, however precariously, within the peace. Bobbie may turn briefly awkward, but she does not leave him; she does not curse him or have him beaten as other white southern prostitutes will for the same revelation (211), and she does not interrupt his peaceful, uncharacteristically loving touch.

For though readers usually think of Joe as resisting love, he does—after a fashion—love Bobbie. After he brains McEachern with a chair, he expects, without any sense of other possibilities, that she will run away with and marry him; whereas with Joanna he is the alienated Joe Christmas we have come to take for granted, and he finds marriage virtually unthinkable. He considers it for a moment, but in a way that only shows the distance he has traveled from Bobbie. When Joanna proposes marriage, "something in him flashed *Why not? It would mean ease, security, for the rest of your life. You would never have to move again. And you might as well be married to her as this* thinking, 'No. If I give in now, I will deny all the thirty years that I have lived to make me what I chose to be'" (250–51). Joe, much as he may seem a victim, at least thinks—though we may prefer to call his thought an illusion or a defense—that he has chosen his pain. If he is not part nigger, he tells Joanna, "damned if I haven't wasted a lot of time" (241). With Bobbie, after he has possibly killed his stepfather, which means at the very time when, objectively, as a wanted criminal, his practical chances for a peaceful life are lowest, he feels a burst of oedipal release ("'I have done it! I have done it!'" [194]) and chooses marriage. With Joanna, at the very time when, objectively, his practical chances for a peaceful life are greatest, he chooses to continue his life of loneliness and waste. We might say he chooses to *end* his life *in* loneliness and waste, first by refusing to marry, and then by murdering again, given that this time he follows the murder with no serious effort to escape his criminal's fate. For again he says those same words, "'I've done it'" (88), no longer to himself but instead to Joe Brown, who can and will repeat them to the sheriff. Somehow, between the scene in bed with Bobbie and his meeting Joanna, Joe has changed, and become as incapable of love as any modernist anguisher in Eliot's *The Waste Land*.

Difficult though it generally is to determine Joe's motives, the source or at least the beginning of that change is comparatively specific: it is the effect on Joe of Bobbie's change. She, more sensibly, and free from his oedipal tangle, fails to see Joe's apparent murdering of McEachern as any cause for them to marry. Instead, it makes her want nothing more to do with him. After the apparent murder, she flunks the same test she had awkwardly passed when Joe told her he was part black, because she rejects him not as a killer, but as a killing nigger: "'Bastard! Son of a bitch! Getting me into a jam, that always treated you like you were a white man. A white man!'" (204). Suddenly, to the only person he has ever cared for, Joe has become no longer a person but a mere type, a formula. Lying on the floor, beaten by Bobbie's pimp friends, with the "two severed wireends of volition and sentience lying, not touching," he can rest "peacefully," for a moment, until the "wireends knit and made connection" (207, 209). From that moment he never finds peace again, unless it be the peace of death, when again he lies brutalized on the floor, again as the killing nigger instead of simply as a killer, after he has "done it" to Joanna as the time before he did it to McEachern.

Unlike Horace Benbow, Joe never resigns himself to defeat. To make his peace he keeps looking for his own niche, an individual identity, a personal code, which to him means simply independence from other people's codes. Joanna, Faulkner explains, does not know Joe sells whiskey:

> Very likely she would not have objected. But neither would Mrs McEachern have objected to the hidden rope; perhaps he did not tell her for the same reason that he did not tell Mrs McEachern. Thinking of Mrs McEachern and the rope, and of the waitress whom he had never told where the money came from which he gave to her, and now of his present mistress and the whiskey, he could almost believe that it was not to make money that he sold the whiskey but because he was doomed to conceal always something from the women who surrounded him. [247]

Joe wants a something, a secret, that is his and not someone else's, but he knows how to assert only through defiance. He tries to violate other people's codes but discovers that, since codes define themselves by their capacity to be violated, every rule he breaks seems to have the capacity to encompass its being broken.

Hester Prynne of *The Scarlet Letter* has the same problem. She violates her society's code, only to find that (as Arthur Dimmesdale knows too well) it has within it a place for those who violate it. Thus in the end she succumbs to that code, though she had tried to build something that "had a consecration of its own" (Chapter XVII). Hawthorne repeatedly describes such dilemmas, and from a complex variety of perspectives. To succeed at making something with a consecration of its own is Owen Warland's small but genuine triumph in "The Artist of the Beautiful"; to attempt it is Ethan Brand's sin in the story of that name, and Aylmer's sin in "The Birthmark."

The world of the unknown that Hawthorne struggles thus intermittently to create, Melville and his Ishmael, with whatever mixture of relish and fear, take for granted (unlike Ahab—or Thomas Sutpen—who is threatened by it). Faulkner takes it for granted, but he also takes for granted that the act of taking it for granted, by himself or by certain of his characters, such as Caddy, Lena, or Ike, is distinctive. Joe in particular lacks those characters' assurance; he cannot fully believe in things that he cannot define. Where by comparison Caddy, Lena, and Ike build their own codes by doing what they want, Joe, more desperate and less certain, builds his—as we have seen—by doing what other people don't want, which to his dismay merely reinforces the codes he means to destroy until they destroy, or kill, him.

In fact, he virtually expects to be killed. He says not only that he is going to do something, but also that something is going to happen to him; for since that remembered but no longer known time when he was not punished after being caught devouring the dietitian's toothpaste, he has never lost that sense of expectation, in particular, the expectation of punishment. And so, when Joe runs away after the murder, though he runs hard and well, he never runs far, and then he lets himself get caught in Mottstown, and then—though he runs off again in Jefferson—he breaks away in a crowd that makes escape impossible.

Hence the critical confusion about whether Joe is passive or active. Surely he is, even more strenuously than other characters or people, both. In effect, he passively watches himself prove his fate by actively resisting it: "He believed with calm paradox that he was the volitionless servant of the fatality in which he believed that he did not believe" (264). Even though he is active in an ultimate sense, as a killer, he passively feels locked into that killing by a past unknown but nevertheless remembered. Locked into a stagnant pattern, he cannot grow, like the traditional heroes of nineteenth-century fiction, or like Byron and Hightower; instead he can only repeat. And he knows—as Thomas Sutpen does not—that he can only repeat; he never doubts that enough even to question it, as Quentin Compson seems to question it in fearing that he has repeated or will repeat the dilemma of Henry Sutpen.

The people in Joe's world (except, briefly, Bobbie, as we have seen), like many of Faulkner's critics, impose that repetitive fate upon him by refusing him the right to be Joe Christmas. He must be either a white man or a nigger (or, as many critics say, a mulatto). But "'He never acted like either a nigger or a white man.

That was it. That was what made the folks so mad'" (331). The role of race in Joe's troubles, in other words, is not inherently epistemological, but it is taken epistemologically by Joe and the people he meets.

Over twenty years after writing the novel, Faulkner, answering questions orally, made Kazin's mistake, seeing Joe as an abstraction seeking to become human, instead of as a human (albeit fictional) resisting becoming an abstraction. The distinction is slight, and perhaps clearer to us today than it could have been to Faulkner, but it defines Joe by defining what about him is so effectively withheld from both him and us. "I think," Faulkner said, "that was his tragedy—he didn't know what he was, and so he was nothing. He deliberately evicted himself from the human race because he didn't know which he was. That was his tragedy, that to me was the tragic, central idea of the story—that he didn't know what he was, and there was no way possible in life for him to find out. Which to me is the most tragic condition a man can find himself in."[7] That is to slight the novel by making it sound as though Joe's essential Joe-ness is tacitly determined by the presence or absence within him of black blood, as though, because he does not know his racial composition, he is somehow more tragic but less human, reduced even to "nothing." Whereas, on the contrary, the uncertainty about whether he actually has any black blood, as Irving Howe says, "points a finger of irony at the whole racial scheme."[8] That irony upsets the familiar novelistic stereotype of the so-called tragic mulatto (as in *Uncle Tom's Cabin*), in which the mulattoes' good sides come from their white blood, and the mixture is designed to make it easier for white readers to sympathize with them. Indeed, the tragic mulattoes often grow up believing they are pure white, only to discover otherwise in some sudden shock, as if to say to white readers: Tomorrow, this could be you. The clear implication is that a mulatto's plight, under the same material conditions, is morally more abominable than a pure black's, and also that both are somehow less good, less deserving, than pure whites.[9]

At the same time, as Walter Slatoff reminds us, Joe is motivated by many things besides his uncertainty about race, especially by his fear of women and religion.[10] Yet Joe's motives, despite all we

can say about them, remain mysterious and form a large part of
the book's distinguishing mystery. Howe suggests that, by refusing
to enter Joe's mind as he murders Joanna, Faulkner erodes the
novel's "tragic scope and intensity," making the murder "too
much an event in the story, not enough an experience of Joe
Christmas."[11] As we have seen, however, the technical means of
such evasion is not only a matter of perspective, of obscuring Joe's
motives by seeing them from the outside; it is also a matter of
simply skipping over the murder, the moment of motive objectified
in action. Like any withholding, this one implies a set of choices,
a trade of one thing for another. It might make Joe's tragedy less
compelling in a classical sense, as the tragedy of an individual
hero, but it makes it more compelling as a modern tragedy of
alienation, the tragedy of an individual everyman too alienated
even to reflect—as, say, Raskolnikov reflects—on his crime.

Part of the mystery of Joe's motivation comes from that sense of
fatalism we have already discussed, from Joe's compelled, unre-
flective sense of having no choice, which would preclude motive
altogether. He watches the hours pass, waiting for something to
happen as if it would happen from the mere motion of time and
not from any act of will, thinking of it ahead of time as mandatory
and already accomplished: "He was saying to himself *I had to do
it* already in the past tense; *I had to do it*" (264). This weight
bearing down upon Joe and forcing him to a particular act suggests a striking if generalized resemblance to Hawthorne's "Roger
Malvin's Burial." Because I find accepted readings of that story
somewhat inadequate, I must ask readers to forgive a digression
upon it to establish the full range of comparison.

In "Roger Malvin's Burial," Reuben Bourne accidentally—and
yet under the influence of a strange compulsion—kills his son, in
what turns out to be the exact spot where he had abandoned his
dying father-in-law to be, Roger Malvin, eighteen years before to
the day. (The day, incidentally, is May 12, the same day as the rape
and murder in *Sanctuary*.) "Roger Malvin's Burial" is generally
read too exclusively as a study of guilt, for Hawthorne's critics
sometimes forget that he is as interested in innocence as he is in
guilt. Hyatt Waggoner and Frederick Crews put the case most explicitly:[12] Reuben feels guilty for Roger's death, projects his guilt

onto his son, Cyrus, and, by killing Cyrus, kills his guilt in revenge for Roger. By thus killing his guilt, he feels he has expiated his sin. Hawthorne's description of Reuben's feelings for his son, however, suggests that Cyrus represents not his guilt, but his illusion of his own innocence; therefore, in killing Cyrus he kills not his guilt, but instead that same illusion of innocence.

Reuben's is a peculiar guilt in that he feels guilty for having done what he believes is the right thing. Had he not abandoned Roger Malvin, they would both have died. Since he is never certain that he is indeed guilty, he cannot repent. To the reader (at least to this reader) his problem is clearer: he is innocent of Roger Malvin's death, but guilty of misleading his wife, Dorcas—to whom he implies that he left Roger only after Roger had died—and guilty of violating his vow to the dying man to return and bury him. But nowhere does Reuben make such distinctions. He senses his guilt, and yet, innocent of the main event, he clings tortuously to the illusion he is innocent per se.

For Reuben, Cyrus embodies that illusion:

> The boy was loved by his father, with a deep and silent strength, as if whatever was good and happy in his own nature had been transferred to his child, carrying his affections with it. . . . Reuben's secret thoughts and insulated emotions had gradually made him a selfish man; and he could no longer love deeply, except where he saw, or imagined, some reflection or likeness of his own mind. In Cyrus he recognized what he had himself been in other days. . . .[13]

He sees not, as Crews says, himself in Cyrus, but his former self, what he had been in other days. Apparently not considering or believing in original sin, in the ubiquity of guilt, he thinks that what he had been in former days consists of "whatever was good and happy in his own nature." Instead of seeing his actual self in Cyrus, he sees an illusion of a lost, supposedly innocent self.

His problem is that he has never managed to forgo that illusion. He cannot acknowledge his guilt because he cannot acknowledge the end of his innocence. Perhaps, from Hawthorne's perspective, because of original sin or inherent human weakness, there is no such innocence. But there is to Reuben, who can see his son as a reincarnation of his own innocent youth. Reuben's problem, then, is that he cannot acknowledge the end of his innocence because the act that seems to have ended it was itself an innocent act. To atone for guilt, he must first feel genuinely guilty; to feel genuinely guilty, he must somehow do away with the illusion of his innocence. He does away with it by doing away with what to him is its only clear embodiment: his son.

At the end we are told, "His sin was expiated, the curse was gone from him; and, in the hour when he had shed blood dearer to him than his own, a prayer, the first for years, went up to heaven from the lips of Reuben Bourne."[14] If Waggoner's and Crews's reading were right—that, in killing Cyrus, Reuben kills his guilty self—it would be easy for Hawthorne to stay within his blood figure and say that Reuben has shed his own blood. Instead, he sheds "blood dearer to him than his own," for in Cyrus he sees not his guilty self but an image of a pure part of him that once, he thinks, made up the whole, an image "dearer to him" than what he has since become. In his confusion Reuben has sinned by not telling the whole truth; in effect, his sin ironically becomes his confused clinging to the image of his innocence. Once he has killed his son, he can cling to that precarious image no longer. Only then, having destroyed his illusion of innocence and acknowledged his sin, can he—in his madness—expiate that sin and pray.

The Hawthornian story of Joe Christmas is not so neat as Hawthorne's story of Reuben Bourne, whose name anticipates the name of Joe's antagonist and lover and victim, Joanna Burden. In coming to Jefferson after thirty years of wandering, Joe too returns—approximately—to the land where he developed whatever it is that propels him,[15] a land where, just as Reuben Bourne imagines he killed a man who was like a father to him, Joe seems to have killed his stepfather. Also like Reuben, though more consciously, Joe feels compelled to kill again. If Reuben, in killing his son, kills not his guilt but rather his innocent self or alter ego, what does Joe kill in killing his alter ego, Joanna? He kills the self that rejects himself.

Joanna's encounter with sex through Joe exposes her to a hidden self to which her familiar self cannot adjust. She is repeatedly described as two people, as at war with herself (219, 221, 243, 246, 248). Her dilemma recalls Arthur Dimmesdale in the chapter of *The Scarlet Letter* called "The Minister in a Maze," where, after meeting Hester (who, as we have seen, bears a resemblance to Joe) in the forest, he nearly explodes with his suddenly rediscovered sinful energy and can hardly keep from shocking by his evil thoughts the good people he meets as he walks through the village. The extremity (by his standards) of Dimmesdale's dissipation is made possible by the extremity of Puritan repression against which it overreacts. Similarly, speaking of Joanna, Faulkner describes her ecstasy of flaunted taboo as the "abject fury of the New England glacier exposed suddenly to the fire of the New England biblical hell" (244). Hawthorne's tone, however, is completely different from Faulkner's in the corresponding passages. Hawthorne is comic, with Dimmesdale made ridiculous by the tameness of the sins he contemplates with such horror, whereas Joanna is made pathetic by the "imperious and fierce urgency that concealed an actual despair at frustrate and irrevocable years" (244). Faulkner gives us the orgies—"physical experimentation that transcended imagining" (248)—that Hawthorne, by not giving us, uses to amuse us by default. Yet, as he describes those orgies, Faulkner still challenges us to retain the ability to laugh at the schizophrenic impulse behind them, thus making for a grimmer and finally more horrifying humor than Hawthorne's.

Joanna pleads that Joe join in her war within the self, but he is baffled and, finally, resistant. Though, from his exposure to Hines and McEachern, Joe is as much a product of Puritanism as she is, he cannot separate out from the rest of him that Puritanism and oppose it to its promiscuous counterpart. He cannot, like Joanna or Reuben Bourne, pit one part of himself against another, except to pit his whole self against the latent capacity within it to divide itself into partial selves. In sexuality as in race (she wants him to be a Negro; 245, 262), he refuses to be either/or. When one side of Joanna's divided self, the Dimmesdale, Puritanical side, takes precedence and she tries either to convert him or to kill him, his response is to kill her, thus killing that urge within himself that would reject himself, that would replace his particular self with a set of bifurcated types, even though he seems to know that to kill her is to submit himself to being killed in turn.

Indeed, the paralleling of a bizarre rhetoric of sexual roles to the novel's much-noted bizarre rhetoric of racial roles suggests that *Light in August* much more than *Sanctuary* can be the central text for a study of Faulknerian misogyny. Critics of Faulkner's women have tended to follow a partly misguided principle of prescriptive realism, and to follow it in a wholly misguided fashion. That is, the test of Faulkner's portrayal of women has tended to be: Does he portray good and realistic women? Most often the suggested answer has been that he does not, that his women are either the castrating bitches (Temple Drake) of one male fantasy or the fecund goddesses (Lena Grove, Eula Varner) of another. Faulkner's defenders, on the other hand, rather than questioning the principle of prescriptive realism, such as by noting that Faulkner's men are as liable to be types as his women, have said that, on the contrary, he *does* portray good and real women, and have pointed to a large number of examples. Most but not all the examples come from minor, less compelling characters or later, less compelling novels.

Perhaps the issue can be approached differently. That Faulkner is far from feminist seems beyond debate, and his chief detractor for that failure, Leslie Fiedler, has composed a brilliant if a little exaggerated catalogue of Faulkner's stereotypical prejudices.[16] We need now to see exactly how those prejudices work in the fiction. In the politics of sexual rhetoric in *Light in August*, the misogynist Faulkner develops a surprising distance from his misogyny. Through the inherent analogy of gender conflict to racial conflict, Faulkner, as if almost unwittingly, develops a critique of sexual type parallel to the book's more widely acknowledged critique of racial type.

His rhetorical method is to spew forth abuse. Again and again he turns to an extreme, self-conscious sexual typecasting that often leads bluntly into outright gender war. The abuse can be comic, as it is early in the book, when the Armstids comment on Lena. Mr. Armstid thinks, "'Yes, sir. You just let one of them get married or get into trouble without being married, and right then and there is where she secedes from the woman race and species and spends the balance of her life trying to get joined up with the man race. That's why they dip snuff and smoke and want to vote'" (12). As Mr. Armstid blames Lena on Women, so Mrs. Armstid, speaking tersely to her husband, blames Lena on Men:

"You men," she says.

"What do you want to do about it? Turn her out? Let her sleep in the barn maybe?"

"You men," she says. "You durn men." [14]

The Armstids, and not necessarily Faulkner, abstract Lena's problem away from her alone, seeing it as a mere small skirmish in a much vaster war.

More extravagantly and even frighteningly, in his portraits of sexual self-consciousness in Joe and Doc Hines and Joanna, Faulkner contrives not just blatant stereotypes of generalized gender prejudices but, much more particularly, bizarre concentrations of the most abominable extremes. Doc Hines's extremity needs no explication. Joanna's is mercilessly a type of the desperate old maid, with even the "face of a spinster" (251), as she feverishly collapses every delight and degradation into a foreshortening span of months. But the full flowering of type and formula in Joanna awaits the collision of her sexual type with Joe's.

Joe is a rapist, only in mechanics more benign than Popeye. Faulkner gives him, in other words, the extremest possible role of perverse male type. His will to rape begins in his intrusion on the dietitian and the intern, which works as a psychic surrogate for the primal scene. That episode is commonly noted as the source of Joe's tendency to vomit before sexuality, and to resent rewards, secrets, and even food from women. For then, at his first and determinant exposure to sex, in a parody of the sexual climax he overhears, he retches forth the sweet-tasting toothpaste he has sneaked into the dietitian's room to swallow; and instead of punishing him, as he expects, the dietitian bribes him to keep quiet, which seems to him only a tortuous postponing of the punishment he would rather have done with. But it has not been observed that that determining scene of overheard sex is also a rape, no less a rape because the two partners are already lovers: "'No! No! Not here. Not now. They'll catch us. Somebody will—No, Charley! Please! . . . No, Charley!'" (113). In response, Joe's own earliest sexual encounters repeat that pattern. Confronted first with an anonymous waiting prostitute—in effect, an unrapeable woman—he feels the sick urging of toothpaste and beats her rather than sleep with her (146–48). The first time that he arranges to meet Bobbie, he envisions her as *"waiting for me to hit her"* (175); and the first time she is ready for sex with him, the still virgin Joe twists their willing meeting into a rape by dragging her out of the road and through a barbed wire fence (178). And so what most appalls him about Joanna is that she too makes herself unrapeable, which is, to Joe's twisted obsession, the worst affront: "He went to the kitchen door. He expected that to be locked also. But he did not realise until he found that it was open, that he had wanted it to be. When he found that it was not locked it was like an insult. It was as though some enemy upon whom he had wreaked his utmost of violence and contumely stood, unscathed and unscarred, and contemplated him with a musing and insufferable contempt" (224).

In other words, it requires a cognizance of Joe as a type of the perverse worst of masculinity to see that Joanna, his double (as their names, both first and last, suggest; for Christ assumes the *burden* of human sin), is a type of the perverse worst of femininity, for she wants to be raped. (Readers of the preceding chapter will know from its discussion of Temple Drake that I make such a remark advisedly, for critics, literary and social, male and female, have long been much too hasty with such accusations.) We might think that Joe's insulted interpretation of the unlocked door is a misinterpretation, especially since Joanna resists him when he attacks her. But her resistance is merely formulaic:

> It was as if he struggled physically with another man for an object of no actual value to either, and for which they struggled on principle alone. . . . Because she had resisted to the very last. But it was not woman resistance, that resistance which, if really meant, cannot be overcome by any man for the reason that the woman observes no rules of physical combat. But she had resisted fair, by the rules that decreed that upon a certain crisis one was defeated, whether the end of resistance had come or not. [222]

In such manner Faulkner, himself writing in a rather silly rhetoric of types, poignantly hedges—or should we call the hedging hers?—on whether Joanna resists Joe that first night. The hedging leaves Joe the more brutally determined to have her his way, but to his chagrin the next night "She did not resist at all. It was almost as though she were helping him, with small changes of position of limbs when the ultimate need for help arose" (223).

And so before long her bizarre pattern of sexual appetite shocks Joe, who until then has reserved to himself the volition for things bizarre. Instead of nurturing feelings particularly her own, she simply goes through a full rhetoric of female sexual types, "through every avatar of a woman in love," and seemingly driven by formula rather than by feeling, "as if she had invented the whole thing deliberately, for the purpose of playing it out like a play." She hides notes in a hollow fencepost, forces Joe to climb into her bedroom through a window (turning him into the Romeo that Bobbie's pimp had jokingly called him), hides from him waiting and panting in the dark house, appoints outdoor "trysts" "where he would find her naked, or with her clothing half torn to ribbons upon her, in the wild throes of nymphomania, her body gleaming in the slow shifting from one to another of such formally erotic attitudes and gestures as a Beardsley of the time of Petronius might have drawn" (244–45). Eros to her is but a sequence of formal attitudes, until, to complete the succession, it dissipates in yet another stereotype, the desexualized, properly admonishing elderly woman, as she turns suddenly prim and tries to reform the bewildered Joe (253–54).

Surely such a pathetic and comic gallop through the range of formulas, especially as it collides willingly with Joe's compulsion to rape, cannot adequately be described by the observation or even critique that Faulkner's imagination is the slave of sexual stereotype. Such extreme and explicit playacting, rather than suggesting that Faulkner's imagination is enchained by the limits of type, suggests on the contrary that his imagination is liberated by a veritable orgy of types. He may have begun with a glib confidence in sexual formulas, but his novel ended up parodying the way sexual formulas can preempt the sexual feeling of love.

The book's language is so extreme that Faulkner's strategy of parodic type must have been, to a considerable degree, deliberate. It can hardly be all by intuitive hap, for instance, that Faulkner links Joe's stereotypical magazine to the worst of both feminine and masculine stereotypes—"a magazine of that type whose covers bear either pictures of young women in underclothes or pictures of men in the act of shooting one another with pistols" (102–3)—in a novel with so much material, from first chapter to last, that matches the very magazine it mocks. Right at the beginning we find the Armstids tacitly arguing over whether men or women are to blame for Lena; then we move to Hightower's being beaten for the sexual crimes the town fantasizes between first him and his female cook and next him and his male cook; then to the dietitian cringing with terror in what Faulkner calls "some burlesque of rapine and despair" (122); then to Joe's raging resentment of all womankind and to Doc Hines's torrent of misogynist abuse; then to Joe's being castrated with a butcher knife and the remark that "'Now you'll let white women alone, even in hell'" (439); and at last the novel concludes with the comic reunion of a husband and wife in bed joking lewdly over—of all things—a comic attempted rape. No other Faulkner novel, not even *Sanctuary* or *Requiem for a Nun*, so persistently and variously turns to sexual hostility.

Still, Faulkner's parody of what we today would call sexist stereotypes is less than fully conscious, and even a little sloppy. He is not wholly free from what he parodies. After Joe beats the prostitute, rapes Bobbie, and repeatedly rapes Joanna, Faulkner can write (in words critics often quote as authoritative) that Joe's "own life, for all its anonymous promiscuity, had been conventional enough, as a life of healthy and normal sin usually is" (246). Such a sentence, in a rare moment of explicit authorial judgment, speaks with the very attitude that Faulkner's plot seems to ridicule. Such moments, though, remain the exception. Indeed, the more one looks, the more one finds that the novel's plethora of outlandish racist and sexist vocabulary (smelling of negro, 313; womanfilth, 121 and 124; and so on, countless times) can be contextualized as the characters' speaking or thinking, and not as Faulkner's; still, some of it remains Faulkner's. I am not trying to rescue Faulkner from the accusation of misogyny so much as to suggest that the human sympathy distinguishing even his most savage fictions can sometimes also direct them, in this case through parody, into something finer and subtler than their evident paraphraseable intent.

Irving Howe makes much the same claim—minus the parody—in his discussion of Faulkner's blacks.[17] Howe's argument implies that Faulkner wrote better about blacks as his career went on not so much because he learned intellectually the viciousness of lazy prejudice as because he wrote better about blacks simply when he wrote better generally, and that the better writing then led him to think better, that is, to turn away from stereotypes. The same might be said for his portrayal of gender roles in *Light in August,* with the further complication of parody, a method that, by the implied irony of grotesque exaggeration, inverts the sexual formula of gender through inverting the literary formula of prescriptive realism. Because in parody a text pretends to subscribe to what it mocks, it might well have begun with the subscribing, even with acting out the uneasy male writer's own fantasies of rapist men and begging-for-it women, before it discovers that it has transformed itself into mocking what it subscribes to.

In *Light in August,* indeed, the parody of formulaic rhetoric works much the same for race as it does for gender—and not coincidentally, for the two are linked as parallel prejudices.[18] Hence, at the epitome of Joanna's orgiastic attitudinizing as a Petronian Beardsley, she insists that Joe fit a racial as well as a sexual stereotype, climactically addressing him not as Joe, but instead as a collective "'Negro! Negro! Negro!'" (245). Joe himself has tried to live by the prescriptions of racial formulas. "Sometimes he would remember how he had once tricked or teased white men into calling him negro in order to fight them, to beat them or be beaten; now he fought the negro who called him white" (212). He has tried, in other words, simply to be white or to be black, as if there were two absolutely separate worlds. But there are not, as the very capacity for mixed blood shows—or the very capacity to be uncertain whether blood is even mixed.

Neither are there two absolutely separate categories of gender personality, male and female. But Joe and Joanna, acting out their violent visions of the worst of masculinity and the worst of femininity, act as if there are. After Joanna has shrunk every hackneyed avatar of feminine love into the odd months out of three years she spends with Joe, she concludes with a pose of pious do-gooding primness, to which she fantasizes she can convert the restlessly

violent Joe: "She wanted him to take over all her business affairs—
the correspondence and the periodical visits—with the negro
schools. She had the plan all elaborated. She recited it to him in
detail while he listened in mounting rage and amazement. He was
to have complete charge, and she would be his secretary, assistant
...; listening, even with his anger, he knew that the plan was
mad" (254). Thus Joanna's orgy of role-playing culminates in an
ostensible rejection of orgy, a rejection of her role as formulaic
feminine sexual victim in favor of an equally subservient, formulaic role as mindless and "sexless" (265) feminine amanuensis.

If, as Joe does from within the novel, we consider Joanna realistically—that is, as a real person actually mad, and not only as a
literary character unrealistically parodic—then we can see a suggestion of motive to her madness. For spinster Joanna (the adjec-
tive hardly retains its once merely objective meaning as the legal
term for an unmarried woman) is repeatedly described as manlike
(221–22, 227, 242, 244, 251). In the social world of this and most
other novels that means she is or is perceived as a woman who has
failed *as* a woman—the same suggestion as in the word spinster.
Indeed, Joanna, in the broadest terms, has had no sexual life before Joe. By that I mean something irrelevant to and larger than
her virginity, for she has had no social life at all, except as mentor
to distant Negro colleges and local Negro women, which, whether
by imposed fact or by racist delusion, is too socially unequal to
count. She lives as apart from the town socially as she does geo-
graphically, so that no one in town knows or even would dare visit
her (48, 81, 275). Meanwhile, as an active benefactor she lives a
life she could well be proud of, but she lives it with zero (white)
social sanction and zero novelistic sanction from Faulkner. The
suggestion is that she comes to see herself as others apparently see
her, as not a failed person but a failed woman, and in response she
desperately tries to act out the full range of roles she thinks she
has failed to live up to. As Joe thinks—Joe who at this point accepts the rule of role for women—"'She's trying to be a woman
and she dont know how'" (227). She succumbs to type, in other
words, as a defense against the excessive *burden* of having defied
type for so long.

In the end Joe will defy type as a defense against the excessive burden of succumbing to it. Meanwhile, when Joe arrives in Jefferson he thinks he knows how to be a man, though earlier he had felt the burden of needing to learn. When he first meets with Bobbie, he envisions her as waiting for him to begin their relations by hitting her, and he thinks—in words that his later description of Joanna will echo— *"She's waiting for me to start and I dont know how"* (175). In the same fashion Joe has tried, before arriving in Jefferson, to succumb to racial type, simply to be black or to be white, instead of simply to be whatever it is he as himself might be.

Thus Joanna, the sexual outcast just as Joe is the racial outcast, tries frantically to be what a woman supposedly should be. She pathetically crams into a short space her mad string of stereotypes, wanting her lover to be what she construes as her superior, whether, as at first, that means beating and raping her, or, as at the last, it means—though he is an ignorant and inexperienced tramp—to manage her money and have her be secretary and take his dictation. And as Faulkner thus fits her to the worst extremes of feminine stereotypes, so he the more aptly fits her lover Joe to the correspondingly worst extremes of masculine stereotypes, making him vicious, uncaring, and brutal, a rapist and a murderer.

But Joe, it gradually develops, comes to resist stereotypes, especially racial ones. In Jefferson he presents himself as Joe Christmas—period, and no longer as Negro or nigger or white man. Similarly, he comes to resist what he calls Joanna's foolishness, in favor of a sense of self unsubservient to type: "'All that foolishness,' he thought . . .; 'all that damn foolishness. She is still she and I am still I'" (257). Then, when she persists in her foolishness, he persists in his. He kills her.

Like Reuben Bourne's killing of his son, Joe's killing of Joanna is meant to be purgative. But it isn't. Faulkner never presents it to us, and Joe never really tries to escape. There is for Joe no solution, no end, no purgation, though we at least see that for some other people—or perhaps we should say for some other forms of literary character, such as for Lena, and possibly Byron—there can be solutions. Such solutions are inaccessible to Joe, who can never break out of that circle he has traveled in for thirty years (321), and inaccessible to us. Lena, like Melville's Queequeg, is a natural creature whose ways are not available to products of civilization such as Joe or Ishmael or ourselves.

We can create false solutions, like Hightower's solution of withdrawal, or the similar expedients of his literary ancestors, Heyst of Conrad's *Victory* and Father Hooper of Hawthorne's "The Minister's Black Veil," who retreat from sexuality into an illusion of self-sufficiency, of privacy.[19] But for them and for Joe, and for most of us, there remain enigmas that finally have no solutions, or that find their solutions outside the prescriptions of type. Hence the countless critical discussions about whether and how *Light in August* is or is not unified seem to fight futilely against its defining residue of mystery, its resistance to formula. Not that we must or can retreat from judgment of the novel or its characters; not that we must finally doubt that Joe is the murderer, or that Hightower has been culpably reclusive. Rather, we must respect, in a world and a novel governed as much by absence as by presence, the precariousness of judgment. The lack of such respect is the failure of Gavin Stevens's black blood versus white blood interpretation of Joe's final acts (424–25), and the richness of such respect is the triumph of the furniture dealer in the last chapter. The furniture dealer knows that what he tells his wife is only what he thinks, only his own interpretation:

> Because do you know what I think? I think she was just traveling. I dont think she had any idea of finding whoever it was she was following. I dont think she had ever aimed to, only she hadn't told him yet. I reckon this was the first time she had ever been further away from home than she could walk back before sundown in her life. And that she had got along all right this far, with folks taking good care of her. And so I think she had just made up her mind to travel a little further and see as much as she could, since I reckon she knew that when she settled down this time, it would likely be for the rest of her life. That's what I think. [480]

By being less sure of himself than Stevens, by being skeptical of type, the furniture dealer becomes more sure of himself. He creates, accurately or not, a finer fiction.

It is a fiction that, through withholding, systematizes the difficulty of interpreting and the inadequacy of formula. For *Light in August*'s showy thrusting of effect before cause again and again from first page to last, its allegedly chaotic disunity, compels an effort to interpret that carries with it a risk of typing. When we learn of Joe as murderer before we hear of his past, we feel forced to ask whether his past explains the murder, whether, in effect, Joe's viciousness is from nature or nurture. The question is much easier to ask than to answer, just as it is for *Sanctuary*'s Popeye, whose past Faulkner added in revision and only in the last chapter, giving the ostensible cause as far as possible after its effect. The murderer Popeye in that way seems to have suggested a method for portraying the murderer Joe. We cannot read so belatedly about Popeye's or Joe's pasts and conclude they are themselves wholly responsible for their fates, but how far we should move in the other direction, toward seeing them as victims, might be and has been much argued. The effect of Faulkner's premature effects, then, is rather less to force particular interpretations than to force a self-consciousness about the problematics of interpretation itself. Indeed, it forces a notion partly against interpretation in general (which itself is a kind of interpretation), and partly against reductive interpretations in particular. And—with a sophisticated reluctance, at the last moment, to give up seeking unreductiveness—it forces a suggestion of inevitable and tragic constraint. Which means that, say, for sexuality and race in Joe and Joanna, the novel—after postponing the reductiveness of decision as long as it can—finally constrains us to interpret. Specifically, we must interpret within the sometimes brutally, prejudicially social origins of language that shape and express understanding, thus bringing the brutality home to a shaping and constricting—in Joe and Joanna—of personality itself.

Our own interpretations of *Light in August*, therefore, should accept that, however symmetrical the novel is—framed by the first three chapters that introduce Lena and then Hightower and then Joe, and the last three chapters that conclude, in reverse order, with Joe and then Hightower and then Lena—it is not unified in the sense that *As I Lay Dying, Sanctuary,* and *Absalom, Absalom!* are unified. But it is no less an achievement, and in some ways more of one, for being made of its particular assortment of disparate parts. Those parts are woven together, with however broad a weave, in a manner that Faulkner did not strive for in the much more disparate novels that followed *Absalom*. *As I Lay Dying* is unified by its concentration on a single family, by the simple narrative expedient of a journey, and—especially where it breaks the journey sequence—by the domination of a single withheld event: Addie's adultery. *Sanctuary* is even more dominated by a single withheld event: Popeye's brutal rape of Temple Drake. *Absalom, Absalom!*, as we will see, is built around the withheld motivation for a single crime, Henry Sutpen's murder of Charles Bon. *Light in August,* with its withheld murder and its withheld motive, gestures toward a similar structure but keeps adding thematically related material that nevertheless has little in the plot to do with those withholdings, which matter so much for our view of Joe but hardly at all for our views of Joanna, Hightower, Byron, or Lena. In fact, as we have seen, even the withholding of motive is glossed over by withholding the murder, which leaves at the center a certain resonant hollowness—in contrast, on the one hand, to the gratuitousness of Popeye's murder of Tommy and the perfect petty logic of his murder of Red, or, on the other hand, to the elaborate preparation for Raskolnikov's murder in *Crime and Punishment*. The filling of this lack in plot, with a more than Dostoevskian vengeance, is one of the things that most distinguishes *Absalom, Absalom!* from the more strictly thematic organization of *Light in August*. Whereas Dostoevsky works up to and then away from the murder, Faulkner in *Absalom* spends the whole novel working circuitously back to it.

Every such shift in novelistic mode carries a variety of consequences. "I have just finished reading the galley of LIGHT IN AUGUST," Faulkner wrote his agent in 1932. "I dont see anything wrong with it. I want it to stand as is. This one is a novel: not an anecdote; that's why it seems topheavy, perhaps."[20] Faulkner seems to have sensed a gain and a loss as compared to his preceding novels. Indeed, compared to *As I Lay Dying* and *Sanctuary,* *Light in August* is much less an anecdote and much more grandly in the tradition of Dickens and of George Eliot, whose *Middlemarch* it resembles in its emphasis on a group of individuals some of whose separate stories barely touch, but all of whose lives revolve around a small town through whose eyes the narrative itself sometimes looks. Though he sees nothing wrong with *Light in August,* in his feeling that it might be topheavy Faulkner betrays a sense that the gain in scope, though it makes for a greater novel than the others, also entails a loss in cohesion. That loss is ingeniously translated into the novel's eerily disconnected power; but nevertheless—if only by the thunderous standards of Faulkner's next major novel—it remains a loss, and of a kind that *Absalom, Absalom!* is not subject to. For *Absalom,* by its intricate orchestration of a world and plot even larger than those of *Light in August* around a core of pointed withholding, manages to be, in Faulkner's terms, both an anecdote and a novel.

CHAPTER 5

Something Happening:
Absalom, Absalom!
and Imagination

*"What was it, Wash? Something
happened. What was it?"* (p. 186)

*What did I expect? I, self-mesmered
fool, come twelve miles expecting—what?
Henry, perhaps, to emerge . . . and say
"Why, it's Aunt Rosa, Aunt Rosa. Wake
up, Aunt Rosa; wake up"?* (pp. 140–41)

In a novel supremely of the imagination, Thomas Sutpen has no imagination. Instead, he is the ostensible motive, the
excuse, for everyone else's: for the imaginations of Rosa, Mr.
Compson, Quentin, Shreve, and for the imagination of the novel,
of Faulkner. But the novel's imagination is much more than the
sum of the various characters' contributions to it. It depends as
well on a deliberately bewildering manipulation of withheld incident and fact: the placement of Chapter V after Chapters II-IV,
which follow it chronologically; the delayed and separated revelations that Sutpen was Charles Bon's father and that Bon's
mother and hence Bon were part black; and, most of all, the delayed and incomplete revelation of Quentin's meeting with Henry
at the old Sutpen place, upon which the whole novel turns. That
meeting, I shall suggest, is the center or imaginative beginning of
the novel, the part that motivates everything else.

Yet it is a beginning we do not encounter directly until the end of the narrative. The narrative itself begins with Rosa and Quentin; and we discover them talking about still a third beginning, the chronological beginning. As a result, for us to sift through the imagination of the novel as a whole, especially as it depends on a set of calculated withholdings, we first have to sort out these competing beginnings, the characters they introduce, and the imaginations of those characters as they contribute to the larger imagination of the novel.

Chronologically, the novel begins with Sutpen, who is less a man than the outline of a man. Mr. Compson senses Sutpen's vagueness when he says to Quentin that maybe the figures of the Sutpen story are different from the people he and Quentin know in 1909, are "victims of a different circumstance, simpler and therefore, integer for integer, larger, more heroic and the figures therefore more heroic too, not dwarfed and involved but distinct, uncomplex who had the gift of loving once or dying once instead of being diffused and scattered."[1] We can hardly agree with Mr. Compson that Sutpen is heroic, except perhaps on the battlefield, but he is indeed—to borrow Mr. Compson's words from another context—of "heroic proportions" (101). The proportions are all we have. Nothing he says to anyone and nothing anyone says about him exposes the secret of his mind, his psychology, his motivation. Nor do we learn anything that suggests he has much of a mind at all. He reaches heroic proportions as much because of what we do not see in him, the simple doubts and fears and troubles of normal people, as because of the grand confrontations we do see, the confrontations with wilderness and time and fate.

Faulkner's procedure with Sutpen is almost the opposite of Conrad's with Nostromo, in the Conrad novel that sets the strongest precedent for Yoknapatawpha and for *Absalom*'s obsession with the past. Conrad regales us with the grand reputation of the magnificent Capataz de Cargadores, and then shrinks him down to human size by going into his mind. But Faulkner never makes such a change with Sutpen. He begins and ends by presenting Sutpen through the filter of his reputation, using legend to build a heroic image, whereas Conrad subverts it to destroy one. The result in Conrad's novel is that we can never comfortably understand Nostromo's trauma, his sense of failure and aftermath, because it seems out of proportion with his famed courage and resourcefulness. Sutpen's sense of failure, by contrast, remains so distant that it hardly seems traumatic. All we know is that he thinks he made a mistake somewhere, and that all he needs to do is to discover the mistake and correct it.

Of course, I exaggerate; Sutpen has a kind of imagination in that he envisions and builds a plantation where before there was only a wilderness. But, as we shall see, his vision is so fixated on a single, imitated, and unrevised idea that by comparison to the extravagantly fanciful fillings-in, rearrangings, and revisings we get from Rosa, Mr. Compson, Quentin, and Shreve, the man who attracts their imaginations has virtually none of his own. Because we are shown just enough of Sutpen to see that there is nothing to him, that he has none of the imagination central to *Absalom, Absalom!*, it may seem that most of what makes him interesting comes from the various imaginations brought to bear on him. Nevertheless, the spectacle of so empty a creature at the base of so fulsome a novel may make it worthwhile to pause over Sutpen's imaginative poverty before going on to consider the more fertile imaginations of the various narrators and—more fertile still—of the book as a whole.

Sutpen tries explaining himself to General Compson. His explanation, like everything else about him, is forceful but—lacking imagination—inadequate. He claims to be motivated by what he himself calls "the boy-symbol," the effect of his having been, as a raggedly dressed white boy, turned away from the front door of a plantation house by a richly dressed house slave.[2] The boy-symbol might account for Sutpen's morality if he had no morality, as he has none with the French architect or with Milly Jones or the baby he gets on her. But it cannot account for his having a kind of morality, unsympathetic and unimaginative though it may be— "like the ingredients of pie or cake" (263, 271–72)—in such things as his settlement with Eulalia Bon or his refusal to drink other men's whiskey until he can return the favor. Nor does the boy-symbol explain Sutpen's insensitivity. It would explain a refusal to respond to other people, but it cannot explain his inability to see anything to respond to. And it cannot explain his proposed experiment with Rosa, or his ill treatment of Milly, both of which are completely irrational, since if he only sleeps with one woman at a time anyway then he saves no time by refusing to marry a woman who bears him a girl instead of a boy.[3] Faulkner hints that the boy-symbol episode is more an excuse than an instigation, for he has the young Sutpen—before he is turned away from the plantation door—fiercely and comically demand to know from his terrified schoolteacher whether he, Sutpen, could really go to the West Indies and get rich, as the teacher said when he read to the class from a book. Thus Sutpen's design had started to form before the incident that he claims inspired it, which shows that the boy-symbol is but a convenient way of explaining to himself his motive for something he already wanted to do. He himself at one point admits "that the boy-symbol at the door wasn't it because the boy-symbol was just the figment of the amazed and desperate child" (261).

Sutpen's ridiculous question to the schoolteacher—he suspects not that the book is wrong, but that what the teacher claims to have read was not really in the book—is about as far as his imagination can reach. Likewise, the salient feature of the boy-symbol episode, since it does not really explain his motives, is the imaginative poverty of his response. Even when he tells the boy-symbol story to General Compson, he tells it without imagination: "'He was just telling a story about something a man named Thomas Sutpen had experienced, which would still have been the same story if the man had had no name at all, if it had been told about any man or no man over whiskey at night'" (247).

Told with so little imagination, Sutpen's understanding of his own story becomes suspect. He explains his shock at being turned away by saying that the rigid divisions of Tidewater society were unfamiliar to him, a boy fresh from the mountains. We need not accept that explanation, at least not entirely. Sutpen's initiation to the cruel hierarchical world seems at least as much the result simply of growing up and beginning to understand the things around him as the result of moving from an environment of frontier equality to one of old Virginia inequality. Only a small child could believe the mountain life to be as utterly without class distinction as Sutpen did. And even in the mountains he has at least heard of the opulence to the East: "'When he was a child he didn't listen to the vague and cloudy tales of Tidewater splendor that penetrated even his mountains because then he could not understand . . ., and when he became a boy he didn't listen to them because there was nothing in sight to compare and gauge the tales by . . .; and when he got to be a youth and curiosity itself exhumed the tales which he did not know he had heard and speculated on, he was interested'" (222). Furthermore, he has been around the plantation for some time before he goes to the big house's front door and gets turned away. By then he has already seen the "taverns where the old man was not even allowed to come in by the front door" (225) and has already begun to learn "'the difference not only between white men and black ones, but he was learning that there was a difference between white men and white men, not to be measured by lifting anvils or gouging eyes or how much whiskey you could drink then get up and walk out of the room. He had begun to discern that without being aware of it yet'" (226). Thus the boy-symbol incident crystallizes an awareness of social conflicts that had been growing in Sutpen for a long time. His seeing that awareness as the product of one incident is a defensive way of simplifying the problems he has begun to recognize, namely, the domination of some people over others, and his own desire to be one of the dominators.

The incident recalls Pip's first visit to Miss Havisham in *Great Expectations*. Pip has grown up in a severely class-stratified society, but he is too young and immature to recognize and understand such matters until he sees Miss Havisham's huge house and meets Estella, who shocks him with the taunt that he is "coarse and common." Pip interprets Estella's insult as an ugly reflection on himself, when it is more a reflection on the society around him and on Estella. He goes home and creates an object for his guilt by telling a string of fantastic lies (Chapter 9). Sutpen, though not so psychologically vivid as Pip, also accepts the insult as a natural consequence of the prevailing rules. But, unlike Pip, he so lacks imagination that he feels no shame or guilt. He goes home and calmly thinks that he can lie, as Pip does, about what happened. To lie, however, would first require imagination and, second, encourage still more of it by giving him just cause to feel guilty. So instead of lying he runs away. In response to being insulted, both Sutpen and Pip dedicate themselves to forgetting their pasts and becoming what has insulted them, but only Sutpen—having no imagination and hardly any psychology—fully believes he can and should make the transformation.[4]

He makes his decision on the basis of his rifle analogy. Instead of applying imagination to understand new experience, he falls back on what he already knows and tries to make his new experience conform to it. "'So to combat them you have got to have what they have that made them do what the man did,'" he thinks. But if he is to get something that makes people do what the man did, then it will make him do that too, as indeed it does. He figures he cannot resist such men—"'there aint any good or harm either in the living world that I can do to him'" (238)—so he decides to join them. Even his manners are aped. He only copies; he has no idea of his own.

> "He no more envied the man than he would have envied a mountain man who happened to own a fine rifle. He would have coveted the rifle, but he would himself have supported and confirmed the owner's pride and pleasure in its ownership because he could not have conceived of the owner taking such cross advantage of the luck which gave the rifle to him rather than to another as to say to other men: *Because I own this rifle, my arms and legs and blood and bones are superior to yours* except as the victorious outcome of a fight with rifles." [228–29]

But when he does learn to conceive of owners as taking cross advantage, he determines to imitate them, to become an owner himself precisely so he can take the cross advantage too.

And so years later he has his carriage driven to church almost murderously fast, in imitation of a rich man's carriage that as a boy he had watched nearly run over his sister (231). When the Jefferson minister protests and Sutpen stops going to church, his need to imitate remains so literal that, every Sunday, instead of going to church he religiously reenacts his boyhood vision of the man who would lie in a barrel-stave hammock with a slave to fan him and bring him drinks. As a boy Sutpen would lie hidden in the bushes all afternoon just to watch the man enjoy his luxury

120

(227–28). Thirty years later, he too lies in a barrel-stave hammock and drinks away the afternoon. He has Wash Jones serve him instead of having a slave do it so that he can bring his former self—the white trash boy who watched the rich man—before him and appreciate what he is by contrasting it with what he was. To complete the scene, Wash is turned away from Sutpen's door by a slave (Clytie, 183, 281), just as the young Sutpen was turned away from the door of the man he later imitates. That man's name was Pettibone. It is no coincidence, then, that Sutpen's first marriage was to Eulalia *Bon.*[5]

His problem is that, having so little imagination, he cannot adapt to things that take imagination to understand. He is threatened, like Ahab, by what he cannot define.[6] Sutpen tells Quentin's grandfather that the Tidewater world he found when he came down from the mountains as a boy "'was a country all divided and fixed and neat with a people living on it all divided and fixed and neat because of what color their skins happened to be and what they happened to own'" (221). But Sutpen's illusory vision of a neat Virginia world fails him when he tries to impose it on his own world in Mississippi, for how will such a description explain Charles Bon? What color is he? Does his color correspond to what he happens to own? Sutpen's mind, bent on seeing things as divided and fixed and neat, is helpless before the phenomenon of Bon, someone neither black nor white, technically understood as black yet socially and economically white, someone who, as Rosa complains of Sutpen, cannot say who his father was, yet someone whose father is nevertheless Sutpen himself.

The inadequacy of Sutpen's mind to explain his experience never leads him to change his thinking. Even the war does not threaten his habit of no imagination. Back from the fighting, he continues trying to fulfill his design, though by then its futility is completely evident. In stark contrast to the changing circumstances around him, Sutpen cannot change. In a world fast becoming obsessed with the past and with the already mythical war, he—war hero though he is—tells no war stories (161). He acts as if there were no past, no record of failure—especially of his own failure—to point to the futility of his efforts or the need to redirect them. How different he is from Nostromo, who, after the silver fiasco, succumbs to an endless feeling of living on helplessly after that part of his life that defines him is over. And if Nostromo *succumbs* to a feeling of aftermath, then, in Henry James's *The Wings of the Dove* Merton Densher *grows* to one. Back in London after his final interview in Venice with Milly Theale, Merton feels an "after-sense" that "day by day, was his greatest reality."[7] Kate Croy perfectly understands the power of this after-sense when she proclaims, in the novel's final words, "'We shall never be again as we were!'" Sutpen too shall never be again as he was. He lives in a world of aftermath, but, strangely, he does so without any after-sense. He is neither paralyzed like Nostromo nor chastened like Merton Densher. He is simply oblivious.

Faulkner gives us this man of heroic proportions, who has no imagination and hence no sense of history or aftermath, and makes him the obsession of a series of unheroic characters who are dizzy with imagination and history, haunted by a feeling that they are somehow lesser figures consigned to the aftermath of what really matters. It is the difference between Thomas Sutpen, who simply tiptoes out of the house one morning before the sun rises and never sees any of his family again (238), and Henry Sutpen, who just as secretly slips back home to die after a forty-year absence. But Henry's imagination, like his father's, we never get first hand. Instead we get Rosa's, Mr. Compson's, Quentin's, and Shreve's.

Rosa more than anyone else (with the possible exception of Henry, about whom we know so little) lives in an aftermath. She is "Cassandralike" (22, 60), someone for whom even the future is the past. Born already an aunt, she has always felt older than her years, as if she were "born too late" (22, 146); indeed, her sister turns to her to seek protection for a niece and nephew older than Rosa herself. "'My life,'" Rosa says, "'was destined to end on an afternoon in April forty-three years ago, since anyone who even had as little to call living as I had had up to that time would not call what I have had since living'" (18). To Rosa in 1909, no one in the South has been young since 1861 (19).

Of course, we do not believe her. She makes that comment to Quentin, who is undeniably young himself. And as she says it she sits before a window where a wistaria vine blooms for the second time that summer (7), just as later that day, when she returns to the place where her own first bloom was cut off, she will discover to her amazement that something else—or someone else—representing that bloom has returned; so that in shock at her discovery—at Henry—this woman named after a flower might be said to bloom, however briefly, once more. And her summer of new bloom is luxuriantly a "summer of wistaria" (31), reinvoking ahead of time an earlier summer we have not yet heard of, the girlishly romantic *"summer of wistaria"* (143) when Rosa at fourteen first fell in love (with the yet unseen Charles Bon), at a time she describes in words that might apply to her as well in this summer of 1909: *"For who shall say,"* she says, *"what gnarled forgotten root might not bloom yet with some globed concentrate more globed and concentrate and heady-perfect because the neglected root was planted warped and lay not dead but merely slept forgot?"* (144).

Young as he is, Quentin too sees himself as preternaturally old, as consigned to the aftermath: "'I am older at twenty than a lot of people who have died'" (377). Quentin does not like to think of himself as young. If his family life, even as little of it as we see in this book—namely, his relation with his father—is a failure, he at least would prefer to relegate that failure to the past, to a realm for which he is no longer responsible, even if he is the product of it. He may be able to walk away from home and never see any of his family again, as Sutpen did; but unlike Sutpen, when Quentin leaves, he cannot manage to deny that he brings his past with him. He is horrified that, so far away from home, even his foreign roommate begins to sound like his father.

His father's response to aftermath is no help to Quentin. Mr. Compson has Quentin's tireless imagination, but he also has Sutpen's obliviousness. He can relish the Sutpen story as field for his fantasy, but he is relatively detached, not nearly so threatened by it as Quentin.[8] He does not so directly identify with it. Instead of letting the Sutpens govern his imagination, as Quentin does, he makes his imagination govern the Sutpens, envisioning Bon as an idealized form of himself. As he sits reclining with his feet on the veranda rail, he says he likes to think of Bon as "'reclining in a flowered, almost feminized gown . . . this man handsome elegant

123

and even catlike and too old to be where he was, too old not in years but in experience, with some tangible effluvium of knowledge, surfeit: of actions done and satiations plumbed and pleasures exhausted and even forgotten'" (95), "'this indolent man too old to find even companionship among the youths, the children, with whom he now lived; this man miscast for the time and knowing it'" (98). Curiously, although Mr. Compson's vision of Bon is but a dream of himself, Bon's letter to Judith supports Mr. Compson's characterization of him, which seems part of this book's limitless, delighted-with-itself bravado, as Faulkner repeatedly returns with some more convoluted second stroke what he has taken away with a first.[9] But such novelist's games are perhaps the only sort of irony beyond Mr. Compson's notice. The letter may confirm his dream of Bon, but it seems to have done nothing to inspire it. He cannot realize how well his words about Bon describe himself because to him the past has no meaning for the present—unless to someone obsessed with the past, like Rosa.

Mr. Compson feels a sense of aftermath as much as Quentin and Rosa do; he is convinced that people fifty years ago were different and simpler. But beyond that mixture of romanticism about the past and cynicism about the present, he is insensitive to the continuing burden of the past, especially as it relates to the real difficulties of the present as felt right before him by his own son. Talking to Quentin, he imagines Henry Sutpen thinking of all women as ladies, whores, or slaves (109, 114), oblivious to Quentin's possible thoughts about Caddy (though in this book Caddy is never mentioned, as Faulkner again plays with us by pretending to be oblivious of her himself).[10] Similarly, he says to Quentin: "'Who knows but what it was not the fact of the mistress and child, the possible bigamy, to which Henry gave the lie, but to the fact that it was his father who told him, his father who anticipated him, the father who is the natural enemy of any son'" (104). Talking on in his easy way, he never pauses to consider the implications of saying such a thing to his son. It is no coincidence, then, that the Charles Bon whom Faulkner has Mr. Compson describe in Chapters II-IV does not even have a father. He has no parents at all, and "must have appeared . . . fullsprung from no childhood, born of no woman and impervious to time" (74).[11]

Perhaps the most moving episode evoking this antagonism between the insensitivity of Mr. Compson and the yearning of his son comes in Chapter VI, when Quentin remembers going hunting some years before and stopping by the Sutpen graves to get out of the rain, where he listened to his father tell about Judith Sutpen and Charles Etienne St. Valery Bon. Mr. Compson, like *his* father, was rather puzzled by Judith's solicitude for Charles E. St. V. Bon. He did not then know that the boy was Judith's half-nephew, and we never learn whether Judith herself knew. Whether she knew or not, her motive for concern was love for Charles Bon, the boy's father—seemingly an inadequate motive to Mr. Compson, ostensibly because Judith hardly knew Bon, but also because of Mr. Compson's own inadequacy. He cannot make the leap of sympathy necessary to understand Judith's love because he himself cannot love.

By the time present of Chapter VI, January 1910, Quentin has the advantage of knowing that Charles Bon's son was Judith's half-nephew; and he uses the information to reinterpret the love his father could recognize but not understand. On a first reading, however, we are not yet aware of Quentin's new knowledge, so that his reinterpretation of his father's story seems not the product merely of a new fact, but rather the product of his more general sympathy for Judith's love. Even when rereading the passage after we have finished the novel and learned the new fact, the impression persists that Quentin can see into love where his father cannot, partly because it is Quentin, and not his father—with whom he has shared the knowledge—who makes the reinterpretation.

Quentin's reinterpretation picks up exactly where his father's version left off. Mr. Compson refused to imagine what Judith and Charles E. St. V. Bon may have said to each other the night of young Bon's sudden return, after a year's absence, with a black and pregnant wife. He twice denied that anyone could imagine it, but his two denials (206–7, 208) frame Quentin's doing just that: "'I was wrong,'" Quentin imagines Judith telling young Bon.

"*I admit it. I believed that there were things which still mattered just because they had mattered once. But I was wrong. Nothing matters but breath, breathing, to know and to be alive. And the child, the license, the paper. What about it? That paper is between you and one who is inescapably negro; it can be put aside, no one will any more dare bring it up than any other prank of a young man in his wild youth. And as for the child, all right. Didn't my own father beget one? ... Call me Aunt Judith, Charles."* [207–8]

Here Judith expounds a kind of postwar nihilism in which nothing but survival matters, postwar whether the war be Faulkner's World War I or Judith's and Quentin's Civil War. Specifically, she pleads with Charles E. St. V. Bon that, since he looks white and has married a black, his marriage sacrament does not matter and "can be put aside," as we will later learn Sutpen has "put his first wife aside" (240). That is the very sacrament that has meant everything to Judith, the sacrament for which, deliberately or not, she has helped destroy her family, putting her wish to marry Charles Bon Sr. above the wishes of her father and brother, and losing both Bon and her brother in the process. The young Bon's miscegenated child is no obstacle to her. "Didn't my own father beget one?" she says, referring to Clytie. But the example of her own father as a begetter of children miscegenated and hence expendable means something entirely different to Quentin in 1910 from what it can mean to someone reading this passage for the first time, someone who does not know—as Judith herself may not know—that Charles E. St. V. Bon himself is the son of Judith's father's other miscegenated child, a child he had tried and disastrously failed to make expendable. That Judith should say such a thing to the off-spring of that child, that she should ask him to call her what Quentin knows and we later learn she really is, his aunt, shows how wrong she is to think his child or any child makes no difference. She tells him to forget his ties to his wife and child, but at the same time she pleads with him to reassert what she may or may not know are his similar ties with her. In the act of declaring certain sacraments expendable, she actually reaffirms them.

She distinguishes his sacrament from hers partly because she thinks his unworthy of him, being made with a woman who is inescapably black and whom he does not love, but also because she thinks it unworthy of her. That is, she cannot abide his stigmatizing himself with so ostensibly outrageous a marriage because, as Charles Bon's son, he represents her love, he represents *her* sacrament. Love is the only thing still worth surviving for in Judith's postwar world of aftermath.

But of course this plea for love is not Judith's so much as it is Quentin's, since it comes entirely out of Quentin's imagination. Not only does he think Judith could not abide the stigma of her fiance's son marrying a black, he also cannot see her abiding a reminder of the miscegenation threat that destroyed her prospective marriage. He never knows whether she knew of that threat, but her love is too sacred to Quentin for him to imagine her accepting young Bon's flaunting reenactment of the same thing that caused her love's destruction.

What happened between Judith and her nephew is not the point. For all Quentin knows, Judith could have known about the miscegenation and not cared. Mr. Compson imagines Henry and his father deciding not to tell her about the incest because they think it would make no difference to her (120, 269), and Shreve agrees in a way that suggests the miscegenation would not matter to her either (341). But neither Mr. Compson, Quentin, Shreve, nor the reader has any authority to conjecture one way or the other. The point is that, whether Judith cared or not, Quentin cares. If her love seems vague or poorly motivated to Mr. Compson or to some readers, it does not to Quentin. Faced with his father's incapacity for love, Quentin reaches out for it all the more.

Mr. Compson says in this very passage *"Because there was love."* But to him love is just a piece of the aestheticized puzzle explaining, by its defining incomprehensibility, the incomprehensible actions of Bon and Judith. To Quentin love is something he misses and longs for right then and there; and he misses it where he imagines Judith seeking it, in family, specifically in his father (and perhaps in the rest of his family, about whom in this book we hear nothing).

Because Quentin thus identifies with the Sutpen story, he resists Shreve's efforts to take it over. "'Wait, I tell you!'" Quentin says to Shreve, "'I am telling'" (277). At that point, in Chapter VII, Quentin has already had a hint of what would happen if Shreve interfered. Near the beginning of Chapter VI Shreve's mocking rhetoric makes fun of everybody else's taking the story so seriously. Following soon after Rosa's unspeakable monologue in

Chapter V, Shreve shocks us, and presumably shocks Quentin, by moving abruptly from things like Rosa's *"all polymath love's androgynous advocate"* (146) to his own "'crystal tapestries and . . . Wedgwood chairs'" (178). Likewise, Rosa has said:

> *But no matter. I will tell you what he did and let you be the judge. (Or try to tell you, because there are some things for which three words are three too many, and three thousand words that many words too less, and this is one of them. It can be told; I could take that many sentences, repeat the bold bland naked and outrageous words just as he spoke them, and bequeath you only that same aghast and outraged unbelief I knew when I comprehended what he meant; or take three thousand sentences and leave you only that Why? Why? and Why? that I have asked and listened to for almost thirty years.) But I will let you be the judge and let you tell me if I was not right.* [166–67]

By contrast, on the same subject Shreve says that Sutpen suggested "'they breed together for test and sample and if it was a boy they would marry'" (177), putting directly, simply, and in almost the three words Rosa mentioned, the thing that through all her rhetoric Faulkner never has her say, even though we can presume she told it to Quentin since Shreve—unless he guesses—can have learned it only from him. But in Chapter VI Shreve soon subsides and gives way to Quentin's memory of the quail hunt. Not until the next chapter does he actually try to take over the telling, thus provoking Quentin's resistance, because by that point Quentin identifies with the story so much that to subject it to Shreve's flippancy would be—as finally happens at the end—to subject himself to Shreve's flippancy.

With Chapter VIII Shreve finally comes into his own. He quickly creates an almost entirely new character, Eulalia Bon, as later he will create her lawyer and still later, no longer satisfied with inventing new facts, he will change the old ones when he decides that Henry and not Bon was wounded at Shiloh, and that Bon saved Henry instead of Henry saving Bon. Quentin's response is a fierce glare, which Shreve returns (299, 303). The glare suggests a sense that Shreve has usurped Quentin's story and changed the rules. Indeed, Shreve's audacity changes the novel. His narrative brings to the same material a different kind of imagination, more free wheeling, less concerned simply to repeat what he already has heard, as Quentin usually does, or to explain, like Mr. Compson, or to marvel at the impossibility of explaining, like Rosa.

Shreve changes the emphasis from what *happened* to the Sutpens to what *is happening*, in 1910, in his and Quentin's imaginations, which includes but is far from limited to the question of what happened to the Sutpens. To Shreve, and to the emerging imaginative coalescence of Shreve and Quentin, the facts of the Sutpen story do not matter: "It would not matter here in Cambridge that the time had been winter in that garden too. . . . It did not matter to them (Quentin and Shreve)" (295). They seek a truth independent of such facts, a flexible truth "where there might be paradox and inconsistency but nothing fault nor false" (316). When Shreve sets out to describe Bon's love for Judith, he invents an analogy comparing Bon's responses to Judith and to a hypothetical cup of sherbet. "'But it's not love,'" Quentin responds (322). Quentin's objection provokes Shreve to elaborate the analogy, but still Quentin is not satisfied. "'All right then,'" says Shreve. "'Listen'" (325), and he tries another explanation, attributing Bon's love to fate. But again Quentin says, "'That's still not love'" (328); so Shreve creates a third explanation, saying that Bon was indecisive and did not understand what was going on, imagining him thinking, "'I still dont know what I am going to do'" (333). By this point all pretense has been dropped that Shreve is describing what actually happened. The interest has changed from memory of the past to creation of it, from completed history to continuing process, the process—in this historical novel—of Shreve's historical novelizing.

Quentin's glare at Shreve acknowledges this change and underlines Quentin's fear of it. For as he and Shreve begin actually to create the story, instead of simply responding to it, it starts to reflect more on themselves than on Henry and Bon,[12] until finally— in perhaps the novel's most audacious moment—they become Henry and Bon:

> Shreve ceased again. It was just as well, since he had no listener. Perhaps he was aware of it. Then suddenly he had no talker either, though possibly he was not aware of this. Because now neither of them were

129

there. They were both in Carolina and the time was forty-six years ago, and it was not even four now but compounded still further, since now both of them were Henry Sutpen and both of them were Bon, compounded each of both yet either neither, smelling the very smoke which had blown and faded away forty-six years ago from the *bivouac fires burning in a pine grove, the gaunt and ragged men sitting or lying about them*. . . . [351]

In the act of making a novel within Faulkner's novel, Quentin and Shreve become the novel they are making, and in turn that process of their imagining takes over, becomes, Faulkner's novel.

In thus giving freer rein to their imaginations Quentin and Shreve learn—and show us—that the story is not fixed or inert, not independent of their own telling of it. Instead, the story becomes whatever they choose to make it. Shreve's elaboration of Eulalia Bon and of the lawyer (from an oblique reference to a legal guardian by Mr. Compson; 74), his three versions of Bon's love, his reversal of the wound at Shiloh, and finally his capacity with Quentin literally to become the characters they identify with all remind us of the fictional status not simply of Shreve's comments but also of the whole novel, and of the engaging nature of fiction as itself part of "real life." Such things invite us, as readers, not simply to watch Shreve and Faulkner *play,* as Shreve puts it (280), but to play ourselves.[13] *Absalom, Absalom!* is preeminently a *participatory* novel, a novel about its author's imagination, its characters' imaginations, and also a novel directly about our own imaginations. It forces us to ask exactly the kind of question that, since L. C. Knights's famous article on Lady Macbeth,[14] criticism has come to forbid: How many children had Thomas Sutpen? (Answer: Five, at least.) The constant placing of effect before cause, coupled with the succession of newly discovered causes, each more plausible than the last—from Rosa's "'without rhyme or reason or shadow of excuse'" (18), to Mr. Compson's octoroon, who is "'just incredible . . . just does not explain'" (100), to incest (265), to miscegenation (355)—force the reader to join in, constantly revising, as the characters must, our idea of what happened. We move from Rosa's befuddlement to Mr. Compson's conjecturing to Shreve's imagining—independent of any plausible conjecture—to, at the end, something else.

To understand that something, we must look at the last chapter in relation to the structure of the whole novel. It will nevertheless remain vague, remain the only thing the novel explicitly calls it: "something."

The whole novel, in fact, is organized around a particular group of "somethings," all having to do with Henry Sutpen:

And then something happened. Nobody knew what: whether something between Henry and Bon on one hand and Judith on the other, or between the three young people on one hand and the parents on the other. But anyway, when Christmas day came, Henry and Bon were gone. [79]

"Yes, Judith, Bon, Henry, Sutpen: all of them. They are there, yet something is missing." [101]

"Judith [must have thought] *I love, I will accept no substitute; something has happened between him and my father; if my father was right, I will never see him again, if wrong he will come or send for me.*" [121]

"The two of them officer and man now but still watcher and watched, waiting for something but not knowing what, what act of fate, destiny, what irrevocable sentence of what Judge or Arbiter between them since nothing less would do, nothing halfway or reversible would seem to suffice." [124]

"Ma'am? What's that? What did you say?"
"There's something in that house."
"In that house? It's Clytie. Dont she—"
"No. Something living in it. Hidden in it. It has been out there for four years, living hidden in that house." [172]

[Quentin] had something which he was still unable to pass: that door, that gaunt tragic dramatic self-hypnotized youthful face like the tragedian in a college play . . . the sister facing him across the wedding dress which she was not to use, not even to finish. [174]

'What was it, Wash? Something happened. What was it?' [186]

"And he (Grandfather) didn't know what had happened: whether

. . the four of them had just reached as one person that point where something had to be done, had to happen, he (Grandfather) didn't know. He just learned one morning that Sutpen had ridden up to Grandfather's old regiment's headquarters and asked and received permission to speak to Henry and did speak to him and then rode away again before midnight." [276]

The peculiar novelistic or narrative imagination of *Absalom, Absalom!* includes one event on which almost everything else depends, one "something" that explains all the others, exactly in accordance with Faulkner's answer when he was asked in an interview how he shaped his works. He responded: "There's always a moment in experience—a thought—an incident—that's there. Then all I do is work up to that moment. I figure what must have happened before to lead people to that particular moment, and I work away from it, finding out how people act after that moment. That's how all my books and stories come."[15] Many commentators call Chapter V, Rosa's eloquent, bombastic, unspeakable monologue, the novel's center. The novel does indeed have a center, but rather than being what we have in Chapter V, that center seems to be—with Faulknerian audacity—what we do not have, the "something" that Rosa and Quentin go to find at the old Sutpen place *between* Chapters V and VI—namely, Quentin's meeting with Henry, a meeting Faulkner withholds until almost the end and even then gives only in the most tantalizingly vague form. In Chapters VI through IX it turns out that everything after that one event, from Rosa's return visit when Clytie burns the house down to Quentin's and Shreve's long evening in Cambridge, is the problem of reacting to knowing what was learned that one September night between Chapters V and VI. And everything in Chapters I through V is the problem of reacting to not knowing it. This one withheld incident motivates the entire plot. The first half of the novel works toward it; the second half works away from it.

Except that the "something" that "happened" is always still happening; we never quite get away from it because Quentin cannot. He tries, through Chapters VI, VII, and VIII, merely to react to it, but finally he identifies so closely with it that he succumbs, not even just to reliving it, which by then is routine, but to reliving reliving it. That is, when finally we come to his meeting with

Henry, we find not his memory of it but rather his memory of remembering it. No wonder it is vague. It has gone so much to the center of Quentin that it cannot plausibly be separated out as something simple and full and clear.

Such specific vagueness (for at least we can say precisely what we do not know) makes for the uniqueness of *Absalom, Absalom!*, even as compared to Faulkner's other novels. If it is peculiar to have the beginning of a novel—the thing that motivates the plot—in the center, as with Addie's withheld infidelity in *As I Lay Dying,* it is far more peculiar to have it there or anywhere else and yet to withhold it almost completely, even in the last chapter, where finally we learn what it is. That we do at last learn that Quentin met Henry, and from that can specify the vagueness, specify what we do and do not know, distinguishes *Absalom, Absalom!* and its compelling characters of ambition and cruelty, Thomas and Henry Sutpen (yes, Henry—more on that to come), from *Heart of Darkness,* Kurtz, and his withheld unspeakable rites. Faulkner is not, like Conrad, trying to mystify us with the vague insidious power of our deepest drives, but instead to shock us, as he did in *Sanctuary,* by bringing the drives out front in their stark criminal reality. The movement from *Heart of Darkness* through Faulkner's earlier novels to *Absalom, Absalom!* is like the movement from Rosa's obscurity to Shreve's explicitness, except that we never lose Rosa's outrage and never gain Shreve's matter-of-factness; for *Absalom, Absalom!* is as full of shocking revelations as it is of elaborately withheld facts.

Indeed, the delayed revelation of Quentin's meeting with Henry is but the largest and most extreme example of a technique Faulkner uses throughout the novel. The point is not to keep us from knowing, but to pique our interest and make us participate in the process of coming to know. Mr. Compson's letter is interrupted for two hundred pages, Wash Jones's summons to Rosa suspended for a chapter. In the sequence of Chapters I through V, Chapter V is withheld until the end, though it comes in the middle chronologically. Similarly, much of the conversation in the time period covered by Chapters VI through IX is left out, since somewhere during that time Shreve seems to have learned things from Quentin that we never hear Quentin tell him.[16] Knowing such things, Shreve becomes—for us—the revealer. Just as he reveals Sutpen's insult to Rosa (177), he also reveals, even more matter-of-factly, that Bon was Sutpen's son.

That revelation provides the third of the four explanations (after Rosa's befuddlement and Mr. Compson's conjecture) of what happened between Sutpen and Henry, why Henry repudiated his birthright to run off with Bon and then killed the friend for whom he repudiated the birthright. This technique of successive revelation, with each new shocking fact forcing a reevaluation of the events, is introduced in miniature at the end of Chapter I, when Rosa shocks us first by saying that Sutpen pitted his slaves against one another like dogs or cocks, then that Ellen saw him do so, then that she found Sutpen joining in the fights himself, then that he made Henry watch, and finally that Judith (and Clytie) *chose* to watch. In the larger example, as we have seen, the discovery that Bon was Sutpen's son necessitates a complete rethinking of the story. The next eleven pages (265–76) do just that. As readers, we are left with the reaction Shreve later speculates that Henry had when first confronted with the same fact: "'"Wait. Wait. Let me get used to it. . . . I must have time to get used to it. You will have to give me time"'" (340). The same participatory process of surprise and revision is repeated when we get the fourth and final explanation, that it was the miscegenation, not the incest (355).

But for most of the novel we see the delay and not the revelation. Rosa cannot explain, and Mr. Compson's explanation is "'just incredible'" (100). Rosa hurries out to the Sutpen place after learning of the murder, expecting to find Henry, Bon's body, and Judith's bereavement. To her never-ending confusion and disappointment she finds none of those. She never even sees Bon's corpse and, as a pallbearer, she is reduced to trying to take the full weight of his coffin to see if he is really in it—a process comically analogous to the readers' surprise at reaching Chapter VI and finding suddenly that the summer evening on which we have been so intent is over, that instead we are in a time somehow the result of the "something" Rosa refers to at the end of Chapter V, though we still do not know what the something is. Such a gap is an expanded form of the last delay, when Quentin goes upstairs to see what has shocked Rosa: "He stood there thinking, 'I should go with her' and then, 'But I must see too now. I will have to. Maybe

I shall be sorry tomorrow, but I must see.' So when he came back down the stairs . . ." (370–71).

Only after learning that the something upstairs was Henry can we understand fully what has been going on since Chapter V. The novel's center, the something around which everything is constructed, is not revealed until its end; at the same time that the second half of the novel works away from that event, in another sense it works toward it. Center and end converge on a single event, the return of Henry, that really is the beginning. Thus, as we have seen, the first half is set in motion by and works up to a discovery of Henry's return; but for the readers that discovery does not happen until the end. When it finally does happen, we realize what we have most likely come to suspect: that it has been happening in Quentin's mind all through the second half of the novel.

Consequently, the importance of Quentin's meeting with Henry, and his reaction to it, can hardly be overstated. Quentin's predilection to identify with the Sutpen story is enhanced and enforced by the old legend's suddenly coming alive right before him. In this participatory novel Quentin, who has largely been a participant only at our level, the level of listening and imaginatively retelling, suddenly becomes a participant at the Sutpens' level, and thereby feels as if he shares the Sutpens' responsibility for their history of horrors.

Faulkner builds the suspense and develops the gothic mood of the dead coming alive and the guilt of the living, the guilt of Quentin, by invoking "The Fall of the House of Usher." Sutpen's house is as closely associated with him as the House of Usher is with the Ushers, "as though [Sutpen's] presence alone compelled that house to accept and retain human life; as though houses actually possess a sentience, a personality and character" (85). Faulkner alludes to Poe's story explicitly when Quentin remembers approaching the house in Chapter IX:

> For an instant as they moved, hurried, toward it Quentin saw completely through it a ragged segment of sky with three hot stars in it as if the house were of one dimension, painted on a canvas curtain in which there was a tear; now, almost beneath it, the dead furnace-breath of air in which they moved seemed to reek in slow and pro-

tracted violence with a smell of desolation and decay as if the wood of which it was built were flesh. [366]

Here is Poe's house as if alive, and the ominous portents of its barely perceptible fissure and its peculiar atmosphere, which, in Poe's similar words: "had reeked up from the decayed trees, and the gray wall, and the silent tarn—a pestilent and mystic vapor."[17] As in Poe's story, someone thought dead turns out to be alive, but that discovery itself seems to provoke a Fall into death and guilt, objectified in the falls of the structure and the family that lived in it. Roderick Usher's and his narrator friend's horror at the end of the one story, with its faintly *Absalom*-like suggestions of incest, murder, and guilt, becomes Quentin's horror at the end of the other and leaves Quentin echoing another of Poe's dead come alive (and echoing also the passage from Shelley discussed in the preceding chapter on *Light in August*), "thinking 'Nevermore of peace. Nevermore of peace. Nevermore Nevermore Nevermore'" (373).

As Roderick is brother to the risen Madeline, Quentin seems imaginatively to become brother to Henry, to become another Sutpen sibling and feel somehow implicated by the Sutpens' fate. Hence Shreve's calling Rosa "Aunt," as if she were Quentin's aunt and Quentin a Sutpen, is just what he wants not to hear. Shreve, however, has a way of saying things that feeds Quentin's guilt. If Rosa is no kin to Quentin, he asks, "'then what did she die for?'" (174). Mr. Compson has already set Quentin to thinking of the whole matter as a family affair, including his own family as somehow partly to blame. He tells Quentin that Rosa chose him because his grandfather was Sutpen's friend: "'And so, in a sense, the affair, no matter what happens out there tonight, will still be in the family. . . . Maybe she considers you partly responsible through heredity for what happened'" (13). Quentin, as we have seen, takes such comments much more seriously than his father does.

But the main reason why Quentin identifies with the Sutpen siblings (short of bringing in from *The Sound and the Fury* the analogy between his relation to Caddy and Henry's to Judith) is that he participates in a reenactment of Rosa's near convergence, after the murder, with the four (the fifth was not born yet) Sutpen siblings: Clytie, Judith, Henry, and Bon. We have seen how at the end of Chapter V and beginning of Chapter VI the image of that scene creates an obstacle, a "something" beyond which Quentin's thoughts cannot pass (172, 174). Rosa describes that climactic day to Quentin in Chapter V, emphasizing her confrontation on the stairs with Clytie. That moment of confrontation seems to lift the episode out of time and suspend it in imagination, where—like Quentin's vision of the words between Henry and Judith, just twelve or fourteen words repeated two or three times—it is continuously present, always happening, never already happened. Though Rosa found at the Sutpen house none of the idealized images she looked forward to, no corpse, no bereavement, and no Henry, forty-four years later she still cherishes the memory of her romantic expectations. The difference is that now she can recognize and ridicule them: *"What did I expect? I, self-mesmered fool, come twelve miles expecting—what? Henry perhaps, to emerge . . . and say 'Why, it's Aunt Rosa, Aunt Rosa. Wake up, Aunt Rosa; wake up'?"* (140–41).

All this prepares us for the scene recalled in Chapter IX. In that scene Rosa once again goes out to meet the Sutpen siblings, at least those still living, again confronts Clytie on the stairs in a moment eerily suspended. This time she finds exactly what she has chided herself for having expected to find before: Henry. Again Henry speaks in a crucial conversation "with twelve or fourteen words and most of these the same words repeated two or three times" (174). The great shock is not just that so much is repeated, but that this time Quentin himself participates; he too speaks in the climactic conversation, in a reenactment of the horrible "something" that until then has haunted him only from a safe distance, from the past, from history and myth.

The few words we get between Henry and Quentin can hardly be taken as an accurate transcript of their conversation, but whatever Henry says, it changes Quentin. His reaction is somewhat like Merton Densher's reaction to his final, similarly withheld interview with Milly Theale in *The Wings of the Dove*. When we see Merton after that interview he too is changed. Milly's words have left him "to his recovered sense, forgiven, dedicated, blessed," so that for the first time he talks of "everything" as everyone else has done all along,[18] and he is far more assertive with Kate. Merton's experience has the power and the authority—or meaning—of sacrament. Quentin's has the same power without the authority or the meaning. Both are changed, but Merton knows better what he is changed to—he can make his decision when confronted with Kate's final challenge. Quentin does not know. He knows only that he *is* changed, affected; he does not know quite to what, and neither do we.

There are many other things we do not know, some of which Quentin does know. But if we knew with certainty everything that he knows, we might be less inclined to appreciate his confusion; we might, at our Shreve-like remove, become—like Shreve—smug. Our confusion about the facts is mimetic of Quentin's confusion when he discovers the facts and discovers along with them that he is an actor in the story, a participant, for it makes us participants too, trying to figure out what Faulkner never quite tells us.

Many readers object to Faulkner's withholding so much. But to do so is to overlook that Henry's role in the novel, the novel's great "something," though lifted from the middle and slipped back in at the end, is nevertheless the novel's beginning. Henry's return motivates the first five chapters, and his words to Quentin—whatever they are—motivate the chapters after that. To deny Faulkner the right to his beginning is almost to deny him the chance to write any novel at all. Indeed, to object to his procedure of withholding is to request an entirely different novel. There are simply some things, like Milly's almost analogous final talk with Merton in *The Wings of the Dove,* that if told would make a different book, things the mystery, the power, the very nature of which depend upon being withheld, as when Sutpen says he subdued the slave rebellion in Haiti without saying how he did it.[19] If we knew how, the episode would lose its defining wonder, its invitation to us to participate, conjecture, imagine.

Imagine we must, in *Absalom, Absalom!;* and Faulkner, though he never lays out the facts, gives us plenty of leads. Cleanth Brooks, in his extensive commentary on what Quentin seems to have learned from Henry, makes a distinction between what Henry said and what Quentin conjectured. Brooks thinks Henry *told* Quentin that Bon was Sutpen's son, and Quentin later *conjectured* three things: that Charles and Eulalia Bon were part black, that Sutpen told Henry about Bon's black blood in 1865, and that it was because of Bon's black blood that Henry killed him.[20] But I think we can conclude that Quentin learned all these things from Henry. He seems too unquestioning of Bon's black blood for it to have been conjectured. He accepts Shreve's reference to it as "information," something that can be known or not known (266). Furthermore, one moment that has not been commented on enough suggests that Henry also told Quentin he had learned about Bon's black blood from Sutpen that night in 1865, and that it was the black blood that made him kill Bon. The same moment, which we shall examine closely, draws our attention to the larger, crucial passage in which it takes place.

This is the passage already referred to as perhaps the most audacious in the book, the scene where both Quentin and Shreve, sitting in Cambridge, *become* both Henry and Bon, "compounded each of both yet either neither, smelling the very smoke which had blown and faded away forty-six years ago from the *bivouac fires burning in a pine grove, the gaunt and ragged men sitting or lying about . . .*" (351). The authority of voice here is undefinable, but we can say certain things about it. The subject, mood, and peculiar transition over "bivouac" recall some of Whitman's "Drum-Taps" poems, especially "Bivouac on a Mountain Side" and "By the Bivouac's Fitful Flame." Yet the difference is striking. Whitman's poems suggest a huge, unexpectedly beautiful army moving slowly onward, whereas the passage in *Absalom* suggests a ragged remnant of an army that even while it continues fighting is reconciling itself to defeat. Indeed, the comparison helps show the extent to which this passage is a voice specifically of defeat, of loss.

In one sense we might attribute the voice to Shreve, because it tells us, as Shreve does, that Henry, not Bon, was wounded at Shiloh. But Faulkner, in a trivial yet pointed joke, has the passage confirm Shreve's idea while denying his reasoning. Shreve thinks Quentin's grandfather had no authority to say it was Bon who was wounded, because he could have learned that only from Sutpen, and Sutpen would not know about it because *he* could have learned it only from Henry, and Sutpen and Henry would not have talked about it because too many men were wounded for it to be worth talking about (344). According to the passage in question Shreve is right that Henry, not Bon, was wounded, but we learn that he is right only because Henry and Sutpen talk about it, as Shreve figures they would not.

So whose voice is it? We can explain Shreve's consciousness as not sufficiently accounting for it because Quentin takes part as well. But it has a third participant, at least as important as Shreve and Quentin, and preeminently qualified to evoke a sense of defeat and loss: namely, Henry himself. Henry's words to Quentin that September night at the old Sutpen place supply the outline of this scene, though—we must assume—not all its detail. Such a conclusion cannot be derived from Quentin's recollection of recollecting Henry's words near the novel's end. Instead, Faulkner gives a backhanded hint right here in Chapter VIII that Henry is the source of this scene.

The whole passage is set off by italics, and all but one of its paragraphs is in the present tense. That paragraph is the passage's key moment, written in a peculiar but meaningful mixture of tenses:

> *Nor did Henry say that he did not remember leaving the tent. He remembers all of it. He remembers stooping through the entrance again and passing the sentry again; he remembers walking back down the cut and rutted road, stumbling in the dark among the ruts on either side of which the fires have now died to embers, so that he can barely distinguish the men sleeping on the earth about them. It must be better than eleven oclock, he thinks . . . . He remembers it. He remembers how he did not return to his fire but stopped presently . . . , thinking not what he would do but what he would have to do. Because he knew what he would do; it now depended on what Bon would do, would force him to do, since he knew that he would do it. So I must go to him, he thought, thinking, Now it is better than two oclock and it will be dawn soon.* [355]

Here we have a present from which we can reflect back on what Henry did not say and, by implication, on what he did say. It lasts for this one paragraph, after which there is the only typographically skipped space in the novel (excepting spaces before and after interpolated letters). We also have, often repeated, "He remembers." And we have a past in which he thinks in the present tense the thoughts that—also in the present tense—we are told he remembers. In sum, we have three different times: one after Henry speaks, from which we can refer to what he did not say; another while he is still alive, in which he remembers the night in 1865; and a third on the night in 1865, in which he can barely distinguish the sleeping men and thinks about how late it must be. The third time offers no problem; it is 1865. The first is sometime after Henry speaks to Quentin, such as the time present of the chapter, January 1910; and the second actually is the time when Henry speaks to Quentin. It is another still partial but nevertheless momentous version of the missing conversation we otherwise have only in the abbreviated version on page 373. Tauntingly—and comically—we learn here not what Henry said, but rather what he did not say.[21]

Faulkner underlines the imaginative centrality of this passage with typography, tense, and a curious repetition of Rosa's and Quentin's trip out to the Sutpen place, the key "something" that by the time present of the chapter has already happened but that on a first reading we do not yet know about. Rosa's and Quentin's meeting with Henry is framed by a description of their going to and coming from the mansion that, as we have seen, recalls Rosa's earlier excursion there in 1865, when she expected to find so much and found so little. Here in this italicized passage Henry conducts the same journey, or what has become the same journey in Quentin's retelling of Henry's words, or what should become the same journey in our reading. It is no more profound than a few repeated details, but they bring out the imaginative identification of the two passages. Rosa and Quentin "walked on up the rutted tree-arched drive. The darkness was intense; she stumbled; he caught her" (365). Henry walks to meet his father *"through the darkness along a rutted road, a road rutted and cut and churned"* (352). Walking back along the same rutted drive, Quentin heard a sound and knew Rosa "had stumbled and fallen," and then he heard her yell at Sutpen's miscegenated great-grandson, Bon's grandson, "'You, nigger! ... You aint any Sutpen!'" (371). Henry walks *"back down the cut and rutted road, stumbling in the dark among the ruts"* (355), thinking about Bon's being Sutpen's miscegenated son, and hence the nigger that's going to sleep with his sister. In Quentin's imagination and the imagination of the novel these are the same scene, framing the same shocking revelation of Bon's black blood. Each version represents Quentin remembering the same "something" around which the novel is shaped, that something that never happens and is done with because for Quentin it is always happening in his own mind.

Cleanth Brooks sympathizes with Henry because Henry, unlike Sutpen, is capable of love.[22] Indeed, Henry's love is crucial; it makes him tragic. But, tragic or not, I find Henry despicable. Coldness gives Sutpen an excuse for cruelty, whereas Henry has no excuse. Unlike Sutpen or Judith, Henry has what Mr. Compson calls the "'Coldfield cluttering of morality and rules of right and wrong.'" By contrast, Judith "'would have acted as Sutpen would have acted with anyone who tried to cross him: she would have taken Bon anyway'" (120–21). Judith is strong willed and loving, Sutpen strong willed and unloving. Henry is loving, but his will is petty. He acts not from love but despite love.

To us, presumably, the horror of Sutpen's raree show, his pitting his slaves against each other like dogs or cocks and joining in the fight himself, is the sheer act of fighting, the particular kind of fighting—no holds barred, and the staggering literalness of Sutpen's complete and unimaginative mastery. To Rosa, to Ellen, perhaps a little even to Faulkner, but most of all to Henry, the horror is all these plus the additional circumstance, the supposed bestiality of Sutpen's reducing himself physically to the barest equal terms with his slaves. In this sense the episode is telling not only for its broad play of character, but also—and more specifically— because it introduces and helps formulate the race attitudes of Sutpen, Judith, and Henry. Sutpen is not really a racist. Judith may even know the truth about Bon; at least everyone figures it would make no difference if she did. But Henry is different. He alone among them can feel such absolute disgust. At twelve it leads him to scream and vomit; at twenty-six it leads him to murder.

Hence it is not miscegenation in general to which Henry objects. It is the idea of intimacy on equal terms, of a black in the *family*, that is, a particular kind of miscegenation. Other kinds, such as those that engender Clytie and Charles E. St. V. Bon, are permissible. Henry has some horrible fear that does not permit him even to conceive, until Bon says otherwise, of Bon's actually meaning to go ahead and marry Judith after they learn that Bon is part black (357). Blacks to Henry are all right to have around, even materially and psychologically useful, all right to sleep with, all right to beget children on, but not all right to have identified with you familially.

The idea of family is crucial; it is as defining to Henry as we have already seen it is to Quentin, which is partly why Quentin responds so strongly to his experience with Henry. Rosa identifies family as the essential thing Sutpen lacks. When Faulkner's editor tried to cancel a passage on the grounds that knowing who was Sutpen's father would not make someone endorse Sutpen's note, Faulkner wrote: "It would in the South. If they had known who his father was, more than Compson and Coldfield would have appeared to get him out of jail. *Leave as is.*"[23] But of course Bon himself is family to Henry. No wonder Henry haunts Quentin, since family is so central to Henry that he must kill for it, but his motives are so perverse that it is family he must kill.

The suggestion of allegory in Henry's fratricide, while not so strong that it blinds us to the story itself, cannot be and has not been overlooked. But commentators on it have not remarked Henry's critical role. Brooks emphasizes that Sutpen does not represent the South.[24] But Henry, not Sutpen, is the fratricide, in a time of national and regional fratricide; and Henry represents the worst of Faulkner's South: the terrified, murderous hate that can overcome genuine love. It is by no means an exclusively southern problem, but Faulkner puts it in southern terms, in a vocabulary of southern race-related situations that—incidentally—are now more national than southern.

Thus it is far from gratuitous that the end of this book centering on Henry focuses on Quentin contemplating the South. The novel begins with Rosa seeking out Quentin, partly because she learns he is about to leave the South and she wants to make sure he takes something of it with him, both for himself and so he can write about it for others. The South represents, mirrors, has helped mold everything that troubles and fascinates Quentin. A typical Fitzgerald character, such as Nick Carraway, goes to the Establishment East from the newly risen Middle West and contemplates in fear that Establishment East. Faulkner's tack is partly the reverse, and Rosa summons Quentin to ensure the reverse. Quentin goes to the Establishment East from the newly fallen (or seemingly newly fallen) Establishment South; once there, he contemplates not the place to which he has gone but—less repressed than a Fitzgerald character—the place from which he comes. He comes from a place, even a home, where love, strong love like Henry's and Quentin's, does not work.[25] Henry is the extreme dramatization of Quentin's own failure raised to the societal level, where the obstacle is more clearly identifiable than in Quentin's case. Not, of course, that to Faulkner love could not work in any given southern family or group of blacks and whites. It almost works for Judith, and apparently it would have if Henry had not interfered. Henry is not the South, he is the worst of the South; and the worst fact about the South in *Absalom, Absalom!* is that, when the test comes, the rule of love gives way to the prevailing rule of race—the rule of fear and hate.

The early version of *Absalom's* obscure and long-delayed revelation comes in *Sanctuary*. There, as in *Absalom*, the decisive details are never given directly, though finally they become apparent by implication. In *Sanctuary*, however, the object of outrage is not—as it is in *Absalom*—a false concretization of a social abstraction; instead, it is irredeemably concrete, of exclusively tactical significance. It is a particular object, a bloody corn-cob, that at last explains how Temple was raped by the impotent Popeye. *Sanctuary* withholds the method of its central crime; *Absalom*, more epistemologically searching, withholds the motive.

Absalom's conflict of motive is dramatized in that passage of obscure, undefinable authority that we discussed above. Henry returns to Bon after learning from their father that Bon is part black. In the cold morning, just as Henry is deciding to murder Bon and Bon knows what Henry is thinking, Bon shows concern for Henry instead of for himself, holding out his cloak and then putting it on Henry when Henry modestly declines it (356). It is a small but moving gesture, parallel to Jim's telling Huck, as Huck paddles off to turn Jim in, that Huck is the truest friend Jim ever had. The parallel is all the more damning in that Henry does not respond to it as Huck does, victimized—unlike Huck—by race preconceptions that remain absolutely inflexible. In *Absalom, Absalom!* the scene lacks the humor of *Huckleberry Finn,* and in that sense is more reminiscent of *Pudd'nhead Wilson,* of the ostensible Tom Driscoll selling his own mother down the river, or of Tom's own fate at the end, when he himself is sold down the river by the friends and neighbors to whom, looking as white as Bon, he has been a peer or even a superior, as Bon is to Henry. It is hard to see such cruelty as tragedy. Only the knowledge that Henry loves Bon, loves him even when he can murder him, stretches Henry's hate into the tragic. It is indeed something like the tragedy of Faulkner's South, where the vocabulary of interracial love excludes the familial love that motivates Henry and Quentin.

Whoever is the source of the scene between Henry and Bon, be it Henry, Quentin, Shreve, none of them, or all three of them, it is imagined out of the sudden juxtaposition on the preceding page, the main source of which is Henry:

> —He must not marry her, Henry. His mother's father told me that her mother had been a Spanish woman. I believed him; it was not until after he was born that I found out that his mother was part negro. Nor did Henry ever say.... [354–55]

We cannot fully understand this moment until we have finished the novel. On a first reading the climax of *Absalom, Absalom!* comes when we finally learn what the "something" was out at the Sutpen place, as Quentin remembers saying *"And you are—?"* and hearing in response: *"Henry Sutpen"* (373). But though we can and should make educated guesses, that climax reveals almost nothing of what Henry told Quentin. On a rereading we know all along that Quentin met Henry when he and Rosa went to the old Sutpen place, so that the moment on page 355, already the climax of the Sutpen plot and of Faulkner's narrative audacity, becomes also the climax of the whole novel. For only on a rereading can we see that it includes both what Sutpen said to Henry that night in 1865 and, however circuitously, what Henry said to Quentin that night in 1909. Together these conversations form the central "something" around which the novel develops. Accordingly, through the expedient of a withheld center Faulkner at first rests the burden of centrality and continuous imagining on Quentin, who lives that center. (Rosa and Henry might be said to die from it.) But once we reach the ending, where the withheld center is revealed, and then go back to this italicized scene, we find what is almost a different novel. In thus discovering how comprehensively the novel manipulates our own ways of reading it, we find also that Faulkner has shifted the burden, the centrality, the imagining, to the readers, to us.

Notes

Notes to Chapter 1

1. William Faulkner, *Absalom, Absalom!* (New York: Random House, 1936), p. 151. Subsequent references to this edition in this chapter will appear in text.

2. Faulkner's tendency to withhold has been noted before. As early as 1939, in what remains one of the best general essays on Faulkner, Conrad Aiken called attention to the "whole elaborate method of *deliberately withheld meaning,* of progressive and partial and delayed disclosure, which so often gives the characteristic shape to the novels themselves. It is a persistent offering of obstacles, a calculated system of screens and obtrusions, of confusions and ambiguous interpolations and delays" ("William Faulkner: The Novel as Form," *Atlantic Monthly* 164 [November 1939], 650–54, rpt. in *Faulkner: A Collection of Critical Essays,* ed. Robert Penn Warren [Englewood Cliffs, N.J.: Prentice-Hall, 1966], pp. 46–52). Faulkner criticism has so far done little to expand on Aiken's ideas. The most interesting related discussions are Jean Pouillon, *Temps et roman* (Paris: Gallimard, 1946), trans. Jacqueline Merriam in Warren, ed., *Faulkner,* pp. 79–86; Claude-Edmonde Magny, *The Age of the American Novel: The Film Aesthetic of Fiction between the Two Wars* (1948), trans. Eleanor Hochman (New York: Frederick Ungar, 1972), condensed in Warren, ed., pp. 66–78; and Walter J. Slatoff, *Quest for Failure: A Study of William Faulkner* (Ithaca: Cornell Univ. Press, 1960), pp. 53–56, 128–32.

More recently, narrative theorists not writing specifically on Faulkner have paid increasing attention to the sort of structures Aiken noted, especially as they relate to disruptions in narrative sequence. To survey the scholarship on this subject would require a separate study. The most important works are Roland Barthes, *S/Z* (1970), trans. Richard Miller (New York: Hill and Wang, 1974), passim, esp. on what he calls enigma; Gérard Genette, *Narrative Discourse: An Essay in Method* (1972, in *Figures III*), trans. Jane E. Lewin (Ithaca: Cornell Univ. Press, 1980), pp.

33–85; Meir Sternberg, *Expositional Modes and Temporal Ordering in Fiction* (Baltimore: Johns Hopkins Univ. Press, 1978), little known and uneven but extremely suggestive; and Menakhem Perry, "Literary Dynamics: How the Order of a Text Creates Its Meaning (With an Analysis of Faulkner's 'A Rose for Emily')," *Poetics Today* 1 (1979), 35–64, 311–61. Despite its interest, disappointingly little of this scholarship can bear any practical relation to Faulkner. Slightly more useful, by analogy, are two studies that apply these sorts of theoretical perspectives to Henry James: Tzvetan Todorov, "The Secret of Narrative," in *The Poetics of Prose* (1971), trans. Richard Howard (Ithaca: Cornell Univ. Press, 1977), pp. 143–78; and Peter Brooks, *The Melodramatic Imagination: Balzac, Henry James, and the Mode of Excess* (New Haven: Yale Univ. Press, 1976), pp. 170–96.

3. Thomas Pynchon, *The Crying of Lot 49* (1966; rpt. New York: Bantam, 1967), p. 136.

4. See Wolfgang Iser, *The Implied Reader: Patterns of Communication in Prose Fiction from Bunyan to Beckett* (Baltimore: Johns Hopkins Univ. Press, 1974), pp. 286–87, especially the quotation from B. Ritchie; also Sternberg. Iser has since treated this idea at full length in *The Act of Reading: A Theory of Aesthetic Response* (Baltimore: Johns Hopkins Univ. Press, 1978), the phenomenological perspective of which seems artificially esoteric and too skeptical of literature's semantic value.

5. Henry James, *The Art of the Novel,* ed. Richard P. Blackmur (New York: Scribner's, 1934), pp. 175–77. Cf. Leon Edel, *Literary Biography* (1959; rpt. Bloomington: Indiana Univ. Press, 1973), pp. 41–43.

6. William Faulkner, *The Mansion* (New York: Random House, 1959), p. 241.

7. Faulkner's actual remarks on James were few and mixed. See, for example, *Faulkner in the University,* ed. Frederick L. Gwynn and Joseph L. Blotner (Charlottesville: Univ. of Virginia Press, 1959), pp. 16, 243.

8. For a contrasting view, see John T. Matthews, *The Play of Faulkner's Language* (Ithaca: Cornell Univ. Press, 1982). Matthews's neo-Derridean study appeared after my own work was largely complete, but my emphasis here on the practical limits of epistemological uncertainty is meant as a caution against his kind of approach. Despite our differences, Matthews emphasizes many of the same issues in Faulkner's fiction that I do, and his admirable volume might well be read in tandem with my own work.

9. Cf. James Wait's calling out his name at the beginning of *The Nigger of the Narcissus,* from which Faulkner also took and made famous the description of human beings appearing like two-dimensional figures cut

from tin. For an excellent discussion of the attempt to understand in Faulkner's fiction, see Arnold L. Weinstein, *Vision and Response in Modern Fiction* (Ithaca: Cornell Univ. Press, 1974), p. 137; see also the comparison of Faulkner to Hemingway, for whom understanding is both less problematic and less likely, in John Edward Hardy, *Man in the Modern Novel* (Seattle: Univ. of Washington Press, 1964), p. 141.

10. See Cleanth Brooks, *William Faulkner: Toward Yoknapatawpha and Beyond* (New Haven: Yale Univ. Press, 1978), pp. 251–65.

11. The most impressive case for Faulkner's modern*ism* is made by Donald M. Kartiganer, *The Fragile Thread: The Meaning of Form in Faulkner's Novels* (Amherst: Univ. of Massachusetts Press, 1979).

12. *Selected Letters of William Faulkner*, ed. Joseph Blotner (New York: Random House, 1977), p. 17, and again p. 20. T. S. Eliot, "The Metaphysical Poets," rpt. in *Selected Prose of T. S. Eliot*, ed. Frank Kermode (New York: Farrar, Straus and Giroux, 1975), p. 65, Eliot's italics. For a good survey of the cultural impulses toward difficulty in modern literature, with a useful bibliography, see William Van O'Connor, "Obscurity," in *Princeton Encyclopedia of Poetry and Poetics*, 2nd ed., ed. Alex Preminger (Princeton: Princeton Univ. Press, 1974), pp. 582–84. See also Richard Poirier, "The Difficulties of Modernism and the Modernism of Difficulty," in *Images and Ideas in American Culture: The Functions of Criticism*, ed. Arthur Edelstein (Hanover, N.H.: Univ. Press of New England, 1979), pp. 124–40.

13. John Fowles, *The French Lieutenant's Woman* (1969; rpt. New York: Signet, 1970), p. 108.

14. For some of Faulkner's remarks on modern painting, especially on Cézanne, see *Selected Letters*, pp. 12–14, 24; Richard P. Adams, "The Apprenticeship of William Faulkner," *Tulane Studies in English* 12 (1962), rpt. in *William Faulkner: Four Decades of Criticism*, ed. Linda Welshimer Wagner (East Lansing: Michigan State Univ. Press, 1972), pp. 18–20; and Joseph Blotner, *Faulkner: A Biography* (New York: Random House, 1974), I, 460. For other discussions of Faulkner and modern painting, see Arthur L. Scott, "The Myriad Perspectives of *Absalom, Absalom!*," *American Quarterly* 6 (1954), 210–20, and Carolynne Wynne, "Aspects of Space: John Marin and William Faulkner," *American Quarterly* 16 (1964), 59–71, which, however, gives no reason to single out Marin from among countless other modern painters for comparison to Faulkner. On Faulkner's own painting, see Ben Wasson, *Count No 'Count: Flashbacks to Faulkner* (Jackson: Univ. Press of Mississippi, 1983), pp. 38–40, 90; and Blotner, *Faulkner*, passim.

15. Cf. the excellent discussion of Faulkner's joining modernist tech-

niques to the folk methods of an inherited oral tradition in Hugh Kenner, "Faulkner and the Avant-Garde," in *Faulkner, Modernism, and Film: Faulkner and Yoknapatawpha, 1978,* ed. Evans Harrington and Ann J. Abadie (Jackson: Univ. Press of Mississippi, 1979), pp. 182–96. If my next four chapters show that Kenner underestimates Faulkner's precision, then that makes the more remarkable Kenner's larger description of Faulkner's achievement.

16. John Faulkner, *My Brother Bill: An Affectionate Reminiscence* (New York: Trident Press, 1963), pp. 148, 152; William Faulkner, *Sanctuary* (1931; rpt. New York: Random House, n.d.), pp. 123–24.

17. *Lion in the Garden: Interviews with William Faulkner, 1926–62,* ed. James B. Meriwether and Michael Millgate (New York: Random House, 1968), pp. 56, 255.

18. The quotation is from a manuscript published in Joseph Blotner, "William Faulkner's Essay on the Composition of *Sartoris,*" *Yale University Library Gazette* 47 (1973), 121–24. The same manuscript has been re-edited in Max Putzel, "Faulkner's Trial Preface to *Sartoris:* An Eclectic Text," *Papers of the Bibliographical Society of America* 74 (1980), 361–78. I have examined photostats of the marginally legible manuscript in the Beinecke Library at Yale University, and I agree with Karl F. Zender (*American Literary Scholarship,* ed. J. Albert Robbins [Durham: Duke Univ. Press, 1982], p. 145) in preferring Blotner's systematic text to Putzel's, which adopts some subjectively chosen readings. Putzel may be correct in following a suggestion from James Meriwether that the last word should read "quickness" instead of "greatness," but the meaning would be the same, since quickness would be intended in the archaic sense, as *life,* and so Faulkner would be claiming greatness for having made his fiction seem to live. (I explain at such length because the matter has been much disputed.)

19. On indirection in *The Sound and the Fury* see esp. David Minter, *William Faulkner: His Life and Work* (Baltimore: Johns Hopkins Univ. Press, 1980), p. 103.

Notes to Chapter 2

1. Notably Cleanth Brooks, *William Faulkner: The Yoknapatawpha Country* (New Haven: Yale Univ. Press, 1963); Calvin Bedient, "Pride and Nakedness: *As I Lay Dying,*" *Modern Language Quarterly* 29 (1968), 61–76; Stephen M. Ross, "'Voice' in Narrative Texts: The Example of *As I Lay Dying,*" *PMLA* 94 (1979), 300–310; Gary Lee

Stonum, *Faulkner's Career: An Internal Literary History* (Ithaca: Cornell Univ. Press, 1979).

2. Floyd C. Watkins, "Faulkner and His Critics," *Texas Studies in Literature and Language* 10 (1968), 317–29, lists hundreds of them, despite what seems his considerable restraint, through which he leaves out many of the most amusing and serious; but we need only recall our own errors to take up the slack.

3. For an account of Faulkner's writing *As I Lay Dying,* contrasted to what he later said about writing it, see Joseph Blotner, *Faulkner: A Biography* (New York: Random House, 1974), I, 633–43.

4. Years later Faulkner came to believe that, though by comparison it had come easily, he had written *As I Lay Dying* too carefully, had known what he was doing too well, and thereby had failed, in effect, by not failing, by not daring to overreach his grasp. See *Lion in the Garden: Interviews with William Faulkner, 1926–1962,* ed. James B. Meriwether and Michael Millgate (New York: Random House, 1968), p. 244.

5. I believe the first to note the problems with it was Walter J. Slatoff, *Quest for Failure: A Study of William Faulkner* (Ithaca: Cornell Univ. Press, 1960), p. 164.

6. William Faulkner, *As I Lay Dying* (1930; rpt. New York: Random House, 1964), pp. 164–65. This edition, based on a study of Faulkner's manuscripts by James B. Meriwether, is standard; subsequent references to it in this chapter will appear in text.

7. Brooks, *Faulkner: Yoknapatawpha Country,* pp. 148–49.

8. Jack Gordon Goellner, "A Closer Look at *As I Lay Dying,*" *Perspective* 7 (1954), 42–54.

9. For a refutation—if one is needed—of the notion that Vardaman is an idiot, see Floyd C. Watkins and William B. Dillingham, "The Mind of Vardaman," *Philological Quarterly* 39 (1960), 247–51.

10. William Faulkner, *The Sound and the Fury* (1929; rpt. New York: Random House, n.d.), p. 213. See also p. 117.

11. The concept and term *defamiliarization* are from Victor Shklovsky, "Art as Technique," in *Russian Formalist Criticism: Four Essays,* trans. and ed. Lee T. Lemon and Marion J. Reis (Lincoln: Univ. of Nebraska Press, 1965), pp. 3–24.

12. The theory of naturalization that I am using, developed critically from the work of Roland Barthes, is expounded by Jonathan Culler, *Structuralist Poetics: Structuralism, Linguistics, and the Study of Literature* (Ithaca: Cornell Univ. Press, 1975), pp. 131–60, 260–62. For excellent examples of its application, which go far to elucidate the theory, see Jonathan Culler, *Flaubert: The Uses of Uncertainty* (Ithaca: Cornell

Univ. Press, 1974), esp. pp. 22–24 and 75–156; and Brian McHale, "Modernist Reading, Post-Modernist Text: The Case of *Gravity's Rainbow*," *Poetics Today* 1 (1979), 85–110.

13. T. S. Eliot, "Ulysses, Order, and Myth," rpt. in *Selected Prose of T. S. Eliot*, ed. Frank Kermode (New York: Farrar, Straus and Giroux, 1975), pp. 175–78.

14. Wayne C. Booth, *The Rhetoric of Fiction* (Chicago: Univ. of Chicago Press, 1961), p. 161.

15. Stonum, *Faulkner's Career*, pp. 108–10. Stonum also notes (p. 112) that Samson, unlike the others, does seem to speak in a particular time to a particular audience, though at what time and to what audience we never learn. He refers to himself as "talking now" and mentions what might happen the "day after tomorrow" (109, 112). Faulkner's breaking his own apparent rules only reemphasizes how close he comes to discarding rules altogether. Thus time in *As I Lay Dying* is far more genuinely achronical than what Gérard Genette calls achrony in Proust, which is but complex or unspecified time, more like the intricate temporal configurations of *Absalom, Absalom!* See Genette, *Narrative Discourse: An Essay in Method* (1972, in *Figures III*), trans. Jane E. Lewin (Ithaca: Cornell Univ. Press, 1980), pp. 78–85.

16. Bedient, "Pride and Nakedness"; and Ross, "'Voice' in Narrative Texts." Though I take issue with them, both of these articles are excellent; Bedient's is one of the several best pieces written on *As I Lay Dying*. John T. Matthews, *The Play of Faulkner's Language* (Ithaca: Cornell Univ. Press, 1982), though it does not much address *As I Lay Dying*, makes a similar argument, asserting (in Derridean paradox) that Faulkner's novels validate the making but not the achievement of meaning.

17. For the notion of literary competence, see Culler, *Structuralist Poetics*, pp. 113–30.

18. For the close relation of *As I Lay Dying* to *The Scarlet Letter*, see Harold J. Douglas and Robert Daniel, "Faulkner and the Puritanism of the South," *Tennessee Studies in Literature* 2 (1957), 1–13.

19. On Hawthorne's dualism, see Richard H. Brodhead, *Hawthorne, Melville, and the Novel* (Chicago: Univ. of Chicago Press, 1976), esp. pp. 38–42.

20. The best discussions of the novel's generic complexity are Hyatt H. Waggoner, *William Faulkner: From Jefferson to the World* (Lexington: Univ. of Kentucky Press, 1959), pp. 78–79; and Brooks, *Faulkner: Yoknapatawpha Country*, pp. 141, 163–65. Brooks's perspective is similar to my own, but by assigning different genres to different levels of the Bundrens (p. 165) he stops short of seeing what I call *bothness*. Certainly

his idea makes an adroit naturalization, but I do not see what such levels are or how they can be distinguished. (Brooks clearly does not mean them as conscious and unconscious.)

21. See the excellent discussion of this subject in Slatoff, *Quest for Failure*, pp. 164–69.

22. That near fight seems patterned after the near fight in Chapter Six of *Lord Jim,* where someone says, referring to a dog, "Look at that wretched cur," and Jim mistakes the remark as Marlow's and as referring to Jim himself. The same novel suggests a source for Jewel's name, since Jim calls his wife Jewel.

23. Several points from this paragraph I owe to Slatoff.

24. The best discussion of Addie's many contradictions is in Slatoff, *Quest for Failure*, pp. 161–62. See also Bedient, "Pride and Nakedness," pp. 62–64.

25. Given his name, his profession, and Tull's comments on his voice, Whitfield may be Faulkner's joke on the revivalist George Whitfield (sometimes Whitefield), famous for, among other things, his powerful voice. See, for example, Benjamin Franklin's account (which Faulkner may have read) in *The Autobiography of Benjamin Franklin,* ed. Leonard W. Labaree et al. (New Haven: Yale Univ. Press, 1964), pp. 175–88. Joseph Blotner notes that Skeet MacGowan's name may likewise be a joke, for one of Faulkner's assistants in the University of Mississippi post office was "Skeet" Kincannon (Blotner, *Faulkner,* I, 92).

26. Perhaps the fullest and clearest example of this obsession, excised from *Flags in the Dust* when Ben Wasson transformed it into *Sartoris,* describes Horace Benbow's hobby of making glassware. He "had had four mishaps and produced one almost perfect vase of clear amber, larger, more richly and chastely serene and which he kept always on his night table and called by his sister's name in the intervals of apostrophising both of them impartially in his moments of rhapsody over the realization of the meaning of peace and the unblemished attainment of it, as Thou still unravished bride of quietude" (William Faulkner, *Flags in the Dust* [New York: Random House, 1973], pp. 190–91). Horace misquotes Keats's "Ode on a Grecian Urn." See also David Minter, *William Faulkner: His Life and Work* (Baltimore: Johns Hopkins Univ. Press, 1980), pp. 99–102.

27. Similarly, Stonum, *Faulkner's Career,* p. 119, points out that Cash defensively refers to the condemning of Darl as an *it:* "It wasn't nothing else to do" (222).

28. William J. Handy, "*As I Lay Dying:* Faulkner's Inner Reporter," *Kenyon Review* 21 (1959), 446.

29. The thought of incest with his stepdaughter (among other thoughts) leads Horace Benbow to a similarly terrified reverie; William Faulkner, *Sanctuary* (1931; rpt. New York: Random House, n.d.), p. 216.

30. Stephen M. Ross, "Shapes of Time and Consciousness in *As I Lay Dying*," *Texas Studies in Literature and Language* 16 (1975), 732.

Notes to Chapter 3

1. William Faulkner, *Sanctuary* (1931; rpt. New York: Random House, n.d., 309 pp. edition), p. 38. Subsequent references to this edition in this chapter will appear in text.

2. Cleanth Brooks, *William Faulkner: The Yoknapatawpha Country* (New Haven: Yale Univ. Press, 1963), pp. 132–33. Robert L. Mason, "A Defense of Faulkner's *Sanctuary*," *Georgia Review* 21 (1967), 430–38, provides the fullest disagreement with Brooks. I find Mason's argument intelligent and comprehensive, but mistaken.

3. He says they are cannibalistic rituals, with Kurtz eating; Stephen A. Reid, "The 'Unspeakable Rites' in *Heart of Darkness*," *Modern Fiction Studies* 9 (1964), 347–56, rpt. in *Conrad: A Collection of Critical Essays*, ed. Marvin Mudrick (Englewood Cliffs, N.J.: Prentice-Hall, 1966), pp. 45–54.

4. See Linton Massey, "Notes on the Unrevised Galleys of Faulkner's *Sanctuary*," *Studies in Bibliography* 8 (1956), 195–208; Gerald Langford, *Faulkner's Revision of "Sanctuary": A Collation of the Unrevised Galleys and the Published Book* (Austin: Univ. of Texas Press, 1972); and Joseph Blotner, *Faulkner: A Biography* (New York: Random House, 1974), II, 604–17, 672–74. I agree with most reviews that Langford's edition must be used with caution. The critical judgments in his introduction are challenging but suspect; furthermore, his text carries less authority than it appears, for he consulted none of the extensive manuscript materials representing stages of the novel both before and after the galley version he prints. A more accurate edition is William Faulkner, *Sanctuary: The Original Text*, ed. Noel Polk (New York: Random House, 1981). I make my references to Langford's edition because it conveniently gives both versions of Faulkner's text in a parallel format, though I have silently used Polk to correct it.

5. All quotations are from the *Collected Works of Edgar Allan Poe*, ed. Thomas Ollive Mabbott (Cambridge: Harvard Univ. Press, 1969-), Vol. II: *Tales and Sketches, 1831–1842* (1978), pp. 207–21.

6. For the psychoanalytical explanation see Marie Bonaparte, *The Life and Works of Edgar Allan Poe: A Psycho-Analytic Interpretation* (1933), trans. John Rodker (London: Imago, 1949), p. 218; and, for a sounder version, Daniel Hoffman, *Poe Poe Poe Poe Poe Poe Poe* (1972; rpt. New York: Avon, 1978), pp. 229–37.

7. On the lovelessness of Faulkner's villains, cf. Brooks, *Faulkner: Yoknapatawpha Country*, p. 339.

8. The only critic to pay more than passing attention to gaps in *Sanctuary* takes a different view, claiming that the gaps make the narrative move so swiftly "that little room is left the reader for prurient imaginings" (Albert J. Guerard, *The Triumph of the Novel: Dickens, Dostoevsky, Faulkner* [New York: Oxford Univ. Press, 1976], p. 129).

9. Cf. Cleanth Brooks's comments on the relation in *Sanctuary* and Faulkner's other works between men's discovery of evil and their discovery of woman; *Faulkner: Yoknapatawpha Country*, pp. 127–28, and *The Hidden God* (New Haven: Yale Univ. Press, 1963), pp. 26–27.

10. Irving Howe, *William Faulkner: A Critical Study*, 3rd ed. (Chicago: Univ. of Chicago Press, 1975), p. 192.

11. Faulkner teases us by never saying here just who watches Temple. Naturally, what later happens inclines us to think it is Popeye, but Popeye has been by the spring, and Goodwin later seems to be watching her (94). Clearly it was not Tommy, because she runs to Tommy as soon as she sees him (96).

12. For Dewey Dell, see William Faulkner, *As I Lay Dying* (1930; rpt. New York: Random House, 1964), p. 115, and also the discussion of her thoughts in my chapter on that novel. For Addie, compare "The shape of my body where I used to be a virgin is in the shape of a   and I couldn't think *Anse*, couldn't remember *Anse*" (165), to Temple's "'I was saying Now. You see now. I'm a man now. Then I thought about being a man, and as soon as I thought it, it happened. It made a kind of plopping sound, like blowing a little rubber tube wrong-side outward. It felt cold, like the inside of your mouth when you hold it open. I could feel it, and I lay right still to keep from laughing about how surprised he was going to be'" (213).

13. The sense of Horace's impotence, be it literal or figurative, is admittedly general and impressionistic but for all that seems no less apparent. He has the "voice of a man given to much talk and not much else." "'I lack courage,'" he says, "'that was left out of me. The machinery is all here, but it wont run'" (13, 16). His wife lies in bed when Horace returns after a long absence, but she shows no interest in him, languidly preferring a magazine. The first critic to discuss impotence in *Sanctuary*

155

was Lawrence S. Kubie, "William Faulkner's *Sanctuary*," *Saturday Review of Literature* 11 (1934), 218, 224–26, rpt. in *Faulkner: A Collection of Critical Essays,* ed. Robert Penn Warren (Englewood Cliffs, N.J.: Prentice-Hall, 1966), pp. 137–46, who on p. 145 compares Popeye's helpless watching of Temple and Red to Horace's helpless watching of Little Belle and her beaux. Faulkner cut from the galleys Horace's remark, "Thank God I have not and never will have a child" (Langford ed., p. 117).

14. See Blotner, *Faulkner,* I, 776–77; and William Van O'Connor, *The Tangled Fire of William Faulkner* (Minneapolis: Univ. of Minnesota Press, 1954), p. 57.

15. For other models, see Carvel Collins, "A Note on *Sanctuary*," *Harvard Advocate* 135 (1951), rpt. in Warren, ed., *Faulkner,* pp. 290–91; John B. Cullen with Floyd C. Watkins, *Old Times in the Faulkner Country* (Chapel Hill: Univ. of North Carolina Press, 1961), pp. 80–83; and Blotner, *Faulkner,* I, 609.

16. Blotner, *Faulkner,* I, 175, 190; Ben Wasson, *Count No 'Count: Flashbacks to Faulkner* (Jackson: Univ. Press of Mississippi, 1983), pp. 76–77, 37.

17. Blotner, *Faulkner,* I, 315, 599.

18. Ibid., pp. 605–6, 617–18.

19. Ibid., II, 940. Gail Hightower echoes the same uneasiness when he tells Lena Grove to send Byron Bunch away because "You have a manchild that is not his, by a man that is not him. You will be forcing into his life two men and only the third part of a woman" (William Faulkner, *Light in August* [1932; rpt. New York: Random House, n.d.], p. 389).

20. Langford ed., p. 44.

21. Cleanth Brooks, with elaborate precision, dates the novel in 1929 (*Faulkner: Yoknapatawpha Country,* pp. 387–91). Edmund L. Volpe, *A Reader's Guide to William Faulkner* (New York: Noonday, 1964), p. 383, dates it in 1930, for the simple reason that Bory Sartoris, who according to *Sartoris* was born in June 1920, is ten years old. Actually, that entails assuming he is only approximately ten, since Faulkner calls him ten in May (23), which, if taken exactly, would date the action in 1931. Bory's birthdate, especially as determined from another book, may seem suspect evidence, but it turns out to be significant when we observe that, in revising the galleys, Faulkner removed a reference to 1929 and changed Bory's age from nine to ten and Miss Jenny's from eighty-nine to ninety (Langford ed., pp. 68–69, 119). Such changes would be consistent with his usual practice of dating books according to when he was writing or revising (for which see Cleanth Brooks, *William Faulkner:*

Toward Yoknapatawpha and Beyond [New Haven: Yale Univ. Press, 1978], pp. 396, 426), if we assume that he did not trouble to realign the dates with the days—which would have entailed exorbitant trouble and expense, for he paid to have the galleys changed and was, as usual, short of money. All this elaborate evidence seems more than sufficient to overrule Faulkner's 1959 reference to *Sanctuary* as "roughly about 1925 or so" (*Selected Letters of William Faulkner,* ed. Joseph Blotner [New York: Random House, 1977], p. 423).

22. Blotner, *Faulkner,* I, 630; see also II, 938–40. For a less restrained account of Faulkner's marriage troubles, see the memoir by his Hollywood lover (to whom we might expect he would have lied even more than he did to other people, but which usually sounds accurate, and is corroborated by Ben Wasson): Meta Carpenter Wilde and Orin Borsten, *A Loving Gentleman: The Love Story of Meta Carpenter and William Faulkner* (New York: Simon and Schuster, 1976); Wasson, *Count No 'Count,* pp. 126–27, 141–49. David Minter, *William Faulkner: His Life and Work* (Baltimore: Johns Hopkins Univ. Press, 1980), pp. 92, 111–12, 116, less discreet than Blotner, insists that Faulkner wanted to marry his wife much less than she wanted to marry him. Judith Bryant Wittenberg, *Faulkner: The Transfiguration of Biography* (Lincoln: Univ. of Nebraska Press, 1979), pp. 89–102, notices several of the same biographical parallels, though she treats them differently.

23. Quoted in Blotner, *Faulkner,* I, 686. Cf. the reporter's vomiting in *Pylon* "as though his entire body were trying in one fierce orgasm to turn itself wrongsideout" (1935; rpt. New York: Random House, n.d.), pp. 109–10. Sex and vomit are also associated by Joe Christmas, and by Faulkner himself in a description of Mink Snopes, "whose experiences until then had been furious unplanned episodes as violent as vomiting" (William Faulkner, *The Mansion* [New York: Random House, 1959], p. 288).

24. The gun confusion is crucial. Many critics miss Temple's error and conclude that, because she is willing to resist him this once, her failure to resist him at other times is because unconsciously she likes him. When she discovers that he has another gun (226), her behavior changes abruptly.

25. Langford ed., p. 116.

26. Brooks, *Faulkner: Yoknapatawpha Country,* pp. 121–26, 392–94. Brooks's explanation is nearly definitive. The only serious objection is that offered by Michael Millgate, *The Achievement of William Faulkner* (New York: Random House, 1966), pp. 316–17, which seems to me to cross the uncertain boundary into speculation too far beyond the text.

Brooks, however, makes two errors that, given the general authority of his discussion, should be mentioned. He assumes (pp. 117, 121) with no evidence that Temple has actually promised Horace to testify that Popeye was the murderer, when the fact that she has done no such thing is part of what makes Horace's meeting with her in Memphis so (in Brooks's apt word), "hair-raising." Similarly, he assumes that, because Horace knows what the Memphis lawyer is there for, he must have expected Temple to show up and testify for the wrong side (124). That would require that Horace expected to lose the case. On the contrary, he had grown overconfident; he is so shocked to see the lawyer and Temple that he has to stop before entering the courtroom, and after entering, cannot even hear when the judge speaks to him.

27. For Faulkner's comment on Gershwin, which was probably a lie, see Blotner, *Faulkner*, I, 754, 107. The passivity is noted by Warren Beck, *Faulkner* (Madison: Univ. of Wisconsin Press, 1976), pp. 203–4.

28. On pensiveness at the ends of novels, see Roland Barthes, *S/Z* (1970), trans. Richard Miller (New York: Hill and Wang, 1974), pp. 216–17. See also Hyatt Waggoner, *William Faulkner: From Jefferson to the World* (Lexington: Univ. of Kentucky Press, 1959), pp. 98–99, for excellent observations on the novel's last paragraph.

Notes to Chapter 4

1. William Faulkner, *Light in August* (1932; rpt. New York: Random House, n.d.; 480 pp. edition), pp. 102–3. Subsequent references to this edition in this chapter will appear in text.

2. The same words the reporter speaks in *Pylon:* "'Something is going to happen to me. I have got myself stretched out too far and too thin and something is going to bust'" (William Faulkner, *Pylon* [1935; rpt. New York: Random House, n.d.], p. 300); see also Harry Wilbourne: "*Something is about to happen to me*" (William Faulkner, *The Wild Palms* [New York: Random House, 1939], p. 204).

3. Stephen E. Meats, "Who Killed Joanna Burden?," *Mississippi Quarterly* 24 (1971), 271–77. Meats also develops an overingenious argument that Christmas probably would have to be left-handed to have committed the murder, but that he is right-handed, finally concluding that Christmas is the murderer mainly because Faulkner said so on the map he drew for *Absalom, Absalom!* The map is strong but external evidence. We must suspect Brown of the murder, but still conclude that Christmas did it. Nevertheless, the intriguing uncertainty remains. The evidence

within the book would be nowhere near strong enough to convict Christmas in a fair trial.

4. See François Pitavy, *Faulkner's "Light in August,"* trans. Gillian E. Cook (Bloomington: Indiana Univ. Press, 1973), p. 40.

5. Alfred Kazin, "The Stillness of *Light in August,"* *Partisan Review* 24 (Fall 1957), rpt. in *Faulkner: A Collection of Critical Essays,* ed. Robert Penn Warren (Englewood Cliffs, N.J.: Prentice-Hall, 1966), p. 151.

6. William Faulkner, *Sanctuary* (1931; rpt. New York: Random House, n.d.; 309 pp. edition), pp. 292–93.

7. *Faulkner in the University,* ed. Frederick L. Gwynn and Joseph L. Blotner (Charlottesville: Univ. of Virginia Press, 1959), p. 72. The yard worker in Joe's orphanage, understandably piqued when Joe asks him why he—the yard worker—is a nigger, turns pitiless wrath on Joe in words much like Faulkner's at the University of Virginia: ""Who told you I am a nigger, you little white trash bastard?" and he says, "I aint a nigger," and the nigger says, "You are worse than that. You dont know what you are. And more than that, you wont never know. You'll live and you'll die and you wont never know"" (363).

8. Irving Howe, *William Faulkner: A Critical Study,* 3rd ed. (Chicago: Univ. of Chicago Press, 1975), p. 128.

9. The pioneering scholar on the tragic mulatto stereotype is Sterling Brown. For a good overview, see Nancy Tischler, *Black Masks: Negro Characters in Modern Southern Fiction* (University Park: Pennsylvania State Univ. Press, 1969), pp. 83–102.

10. Walter J. Slatoff, *Quest for Failure: A Study of William Faulkner* (Ithaca: Cornell Univ. Press, 1960), pp. 179–86.

11. Howe, *Faulkner,* p. 204.

12. Hyatt H. Waggoner, *Hawthorne: A Critical Study,* 2nd ed. (Cambridge: Harvard Univ. Press, 1963), p. 97; Frederick C. Crews, *The Sins of the Fathers: Hawthorne's Psychological Themes* (New York: Oxford Univ. Press, 1966), pp. 87–88.

13. Nathaniel Hawthorne, *Mosses from an Old Manse,* ed. William Charvat et al. (1846; rpt. Athens: Ohio Univ. Press, 1974), p. 351.

14. Ibid., p. 360.

15. Some critics hastily assume that the Hineses (before moving to Mottstown) or the McEacherns live in Yoknapatawpha or even in Jefferson. Clearly they do not, though the Hineses live within a modest distance of Memphis and the McEacherns somewhere south of it (180, 181). For a description of the town near the McEacherns, clearly not Jefferson, see p. 162.

16. Leslie A. Fiedler, *Love and Death in the American Novel,* rev. ed.

(New York: Stein and Day, 1966), esp. pp. 320–25 (where, however, Fiedler mixes up scenes from *Sanctuary*). For a defense of Faulkner on women, see Sally R. Page, *Faulkner's Women: Characterization and Meaning* (Deland, Fla.: Everett/Edwards, 1972).

17. "Faulkner and the Negroes," in Howe, *Faulkner*, pp. 116–37, which, though largely ignored, seems to me the best treatment of its subject.

18. See Thadious M. Davis, *Faulkner's "Negro": Art and the Southern Context* (Baton Rouge: Louisiana State Univ. Press, 1983), pp. 140–42.

19. See esp. p. 63, where Hightower tries to cover his face like Hooper, and where Faulkner describes him in exaggerated, Hawthornesque terms.

20. *Selected Letters of William Faulkner,* ed. Joseph Blotner (New York: Random House, 1977), p. 66.

Notes to Chapter 5

1. William Faulkner, *Absalom, Absalom!* (New York: Random House, 1936), p. 89. Subsequent references to this edition will appear in text.

2. One source for the boy-symbol seems to be the confrontation between Matthew Maule and Black Scipio in *The House of the Seven Gables* (Ch. XIII). And the poignant excursion of Clifford and Hepzibah late in the same novel (Ch. XVII) seems to contribute to the more fanatical escapade of Doc and Mrs. Hines late in *Light in August*. Still, I agree with Michael Millgate that the comparisons sometimes suggested between *The House of the Seven Gables* and *Absalom* are too general (*The Achievement of William Faulkner* [New York: Random House, 1966], pp. 162–63).

3. At least that's so as far as I can see; oddly, no one seems to have commented on it. It could be an error on Faulkner's part, and not just on Sutpen's. Brooks seems to make the same mistake when he jokes that "What the aging Sutpen really needed to improve his chances was an easy and quick system of divorce which would allow him to change wives legally once or twice more, if need be, in order to get a male heir" (Brooks, *William Faulkner: The Yoknapatawpha Country* [New Haven: Yale Univ. Press, 1963], p. 442). But a new wife is no more or less likely to bear Sutpen a male heir than the wife she replaces. The odds are the same with one woman as with another, unless either can bear no children at all.

4. For an interesting but I think strained view of Sutpen as more psy-

chologically evoked, see T. H. Adamowski, "Children of the Idea: Heroes and Family Romances in *Absalom, Absalom!*," *Mosaic* 10 (1976), 115–31.

5. I assume that Sutpen's first wife's maiden name was Bon, which Mr. Compson does not assume, but which the chronology does (265–66, 381). Perhaps, as Brooks observes, Faulkner goofed (*Faulkner: Yoknapatawpha Country*, pp. 425–26).

6. For other similarities between Sutpen and Ahab, see Richard P. Adams, "The Apprenticeship of William Faulkner," *Tulane Studies in English* 12 (1962), rpt. in *William Faulkner: Four Decades of Criticism*, ed. Linda Welshimer Wagner (East Lansing: Michigan State Univ. Press, 1972), p. 34.

7. Henry James, *The Wings of the Dove* (1902; rpt. New York: Scribner's, 1909), II, 337.

8. On Mr. Compson's detachment, see Arthur F. Kinney, *Faulkner's Narrative Poetics: Style as Vision* (Amherst: Univ. of Massachusetts Press, 1978), pp. 203–5. Though Kinney also notes that, especially if we consider what we learn about Mr. Compson in *The Sound and the Fury* and what we learn about his ancestors in the Appendix that Faulkner added to *The Sound and the Fury* ten years after writing *Absalom,* then we can see ways that Mr. Compson *is* threatened by Sutpen, whose rise from poverty exposes the shallowness of Mr. Compson's crumbling aristocratic pretensions.

9. Donald M. Kartiganer, *The Fragile Thread: The Meaning of Form in Faulkner's Novels* (Amherst: Univ. of Massachusetts Press, 1979), argues more broadly and from different evidence for the same view of Mr. Compson's Bon as a wish fulfillment. On a smaller point, it might be noted that Kartiganer also says the letter reveals a different Bon from Mr. Compson's version. He contends that Mr. Compson imagines Bon's letters as foppish, which this one is not. But Mr. Compson clearly differentiates this letter from the others (128–29), and it reveals exactly the aesthete and fatalist he has so elaborately envisioned. (To make things yet more complicated, that there were other letters at all is only Mr. Compson's speculation; Shreve sometimes agrees [326, 343], sometimes disagrees [325], and sometimes can't decide [332].) For another and excellent reading of how Mr. Compson's, Quentin's, and Shreve's biases shape their perspectives, see John T. Matthews, *The Play of Faulkner's Language* (Ithaca: Cornell Univ. Press, 1982), pp. 134–48. On Mr. Compson's projection of his own misogyny onto Sutpen, see Hugh M. Ruppersburg, *Voice and Eye in Faulkner's Fiction* (Athens: Univ. of Georgia Press, 1983), p. 107.

10. Faulkner wrote his editor in 1934 that he used Quentin in *Absalom* "because it is just before he is to commit suicide because of his sister" (*Selected Letters of William Faulkner,* ed. Joseph Blotner [New York: Random House, 1979], p. 79). Two books study, and perhaps exaggerate, the links between *Absalom, Absalom!* and *The Sound and the Fury:* John T. Irwin, *Doubling and Incest/Repetition and Revenge: A Speculative Reading of Faulkner* (Baltimore: Johns Hopkins Univ. Press, 1975), and Estella Schoenberg, *Old Tales and Talking: Quentin Compson in William Faulkner's "Absalom, Absalom!" and Related Works* (Jackson: Univ. Press of Mississippi, 1977).

11. Faulkner's own weak father and the weak parents throughout his fiction are a major theme in David Minter, *William Faulkner: His Life and Work* (Baltimore: Johns Hopkins Univ. Press, 1980). Sutpen began to notice the world's variety only after his mother died and left him to his shiftless father (pp. 223ff.). On Quentin's frustrated desire for his father's love, see Irwin, *Doubling and Incest,* pp. 47–50. Incidentally, Mr. Compson's fascination with the octoroon has a source in Faulkner's family history. Faulkner's grandfather deserted his wife (Damuddy, the model for Quentin's grandmother), apparently to run off with an octoroon (Joseph Blotner, *Faulkner: A Biography* [New York: Random House, 1974], I, 57).

12. Irwin's is the most interesting study of Quentin's identification with the Sutpen story, though his fascinating book must be read skeptically, as its subtitle *(A Speculative Reading)* concedes.

13. The notion of readers' participation in the texts they confront has become fairly common in recent years, but Faulkner's fiction, and *Absalom* most of all, carries the routine participation of readers far beyond the general principles that apply to all texts. See especially Kinney's discussion of what he calls "constitutive consciousness" (*Faulkner's Narrative Poetics,* passim).

14. L. C. Knights, "How Many Children Had Lady Macbeth?: An Essay in the Theory and Practice of Shakespeare Criticism," in *Explorations* (1947; rpt. New York: New York Univ. Press, 1964), pp. 15–54.

15. *Lion in the Garden: Interviews with William Faulkner,* ed. James B. Meriwether and Michael Millgate (New York: Random House, 1968), p. 220.

16. Brooks, *Faulkner: Yoknapatawpha Country,* p. 323, and *William Faulkner: Toward Yoknapatawpha and Beyond* (New Haven: Yale Univ. Press, 1978), pp. 311–14.

17. *Collected Works of Edgar Allan Poe,* ed. Thomas Ollive Mabbott (Cambridge: Harvard Univ. Press, 1969-), II: *Tales and Sketches, 1831-*

1842, (1978), pp. 399–400. For another parallel between Poe's story and Faulkner's, see Adams, "The Apprenticeship of William Faulkner," p. 31.

18. James, *The Wings of the Dove*, II, 343. For a discussion of "everything" in James, as opposed to "something," see William A. Freedman, "Universality in 'The Jolly Corner,'" *Texas Studies in Language and Literature* 4 (Spring 1962), 12–15.

19. Especially since by then there were no slaves in Haiti. Again, we can only conjecture whether the error is Faulkner's or his characters'.

20. Brooks, *Faulkner: Toward Yoknapatawpha and Beyond,* pp. 301–28. This is curiously inconsistent with the argument in Brooks's earlier book, where he does not make so great a distinction: "Faulkner has made it quite plain, however, that Bon's possession of Negro blood was more than a mere conjecture made by Quentin and Shreve. It was evidently something that Quentin discovered" (*Faulkner: Yoknapatawpha Country*, p. 437).

21. Two articles precede me in noticing Henry's peculiar presence here, reading the passage less closely and drawing somewhat different conclusions that I cannot quite concur with: Carl E. Rollyson, Jr., "The Re-creation of the Past in *Absalom, Absalom!*," *Mississippi Quarterly* 29 (1976), 369; Claudia Brodsky, "The Working of Narrative in *Absalom, Absalom!*: A Textual Analysis," *Amerikastudien/American Studies* 23 (1978), 252–55. The differences among our readings are much too technical to elaborate here, and interested readers would do best to examine the other treatments for themselves. That we independently noticed the significance of the phrase *"Nor did Henry ever say"* (along with several other recent commentators who merely mention it) reinforces our sense of its distinctiveness. Other discussions of the same problem that miss or ignore that phrase must resort to more subjectively selected evidence.

22. Brooks, *Faulkner: Yoknapatawpha Country,* pp. 303, 305, 318–19. There is even a well-received argument by a respected Faulknerian that Henry was right to kill Bon: M. E. Bradford, "Brother, Son, and Heir: The Structural Focus of Faulkner's *Absalom, Absalom!*," *Sewanee Review* 78 (1970), 76–98. It will be seen that my argument is diametrically opposed to Bradford's, who praises Judith—on account of her loyalty—for the same unconsummated wish (to marry Bon) for which he thinks Bon deserves vigilante capital punishment. But perhaps Bradford's idea is only less subtle than Brooks's remark that Henry's "role" is "thrust upon him by circumstance" (p. 336), or than the claim that "Charles actually gives Henry no alternative" (Edmund Volpe, *A Reader's Guide to William Faulkner* [New York: Noonday, 1964], p. 209).

23. Blotner, *Faulkner,* II, 937.

24. Brooks, *Faulkner: Yoknapatawpha Country,* pp. 426–28; also *Faulkner: Toward Yoknapatawpha and Beyond,* pp. 283–300. For a tempting rebuttal, see Carolyn Porter, *Seeing and Being: The Plight of the Participant Observer in Emerson, James, Adams, and Faulkner* (Middletown, Conn.: Wesleyan Univ. Press, 1981), pp. 207–40.

25. I call Quentin's love strong, despite the intriguing but revisionist 1946 Appendix to *The Sound and the Fury,* where Faulkner says that Quentin "loved only death" (rpt. in William Faulkner, *The Sound and the Fury* [1929; rpt. New York: Random House, n.d.], p. 411). For a comparison of Sutpen to Jay Gatsby, see Cleanth Brooks, "The American 'Innocence' in James, Fitzgerald and Faulkner," in *A Shaping Joy: Studies in the Writer's Craft* (London: Methuen, 1971), pp. 181–97.

Index

Index

Index